THREE ESSAYS

ON

SHAKESPEARE'S TRAGEDY

OF

KING LEAR.

BY PUPILS OF THE CITY OF LONDON SCHOOL.

LONDON:

BRUCE AND FORD, PRINTERS,

TRUMP STREET, KING STREET, CHEAPSIDE.

1851.

CONTENTS.

ESSAY I.

ESSAY II.

ESSAY III.

ESSAY I.

A PARALLEL

BETWEEN

SHAKESPEARE'S

TRAGEDY OF KING LEAR

AND

THE ŒDIPUS IN COLONO

OF SOPHOCLES;

STATING THE GENERAL DESIGN OF EACH PLAY, AND CONTRASTING THE CHARACTERS INTRODUCED, IN THEIR POINTS OF SIMILARITY AND DISSIMILARITY.

"Χω μεν παιδες ἀειδον, ὁ δαίπολος ἤθελε κριναι."—*Theoc.*

BY JOHN ROBERT SEELEY.

ESSAY I.

CHAPTER I.

I CONCEIVE that in the subject proposed, the comparison is not so much between two poets as between two systems. Had Æschylus been put in opposition to Sophocles, it would have been for us to have decided, as those judges would have done who, in ancient times at the feast of Bacchus, weighed the merits of the contending bards, and adjudged the ivy-wreath. Or had Webster's Duchess of Amalfi been brought into comparison with King Lear, the question would still have been one of individual merit. But when a poem composed by the military compeer of Pericles for the applause of a generation which had seen that mighty statesman on the bema* and followed him to the field—a poem preserved in mouldy manuscripts during eighteen centuries, and rescued from an oblivion deep as the grave, at a period when the British stage was but beginning its career, is compared with a drama of the Elizabethan age, which has never been absent from the theatre, and which time has not yet antiquated, the question becomes

* The orator's platform.

B

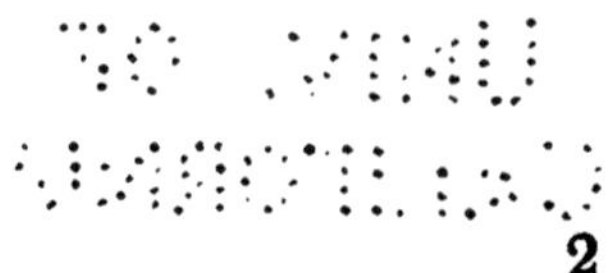

immeasurably wider. We are no longer comparing Shakespeare with Sophocles, but modern art with ancient, Britain with Attica, Christianity with Paganism. Is there, then, no difference of design, of principle, of dramatic art, concealed under the superficial coincidence of a dialogical form, and a so-called tragical conclusion? Many such differences undoubtedly there are, and that not merely in the detail or the unimportant machinery of the plot, or in the trifling discrepancies of metre and diction, but in the moral of the piece, in the conception of character, in the degree of imitation of life, in fact, in every point of moment wherein any difference could rationally be conceived to exist. And yet the Greek drama and our own are not altogether heterogeneous creations. The points of divergence are neither capricious nor unaccountable, nor is it difficult to discern a law in them; where there is not identity there is commonly analogy. These analogies and dissimilarities could scarcely be better traced and illustrated than by a parallel between two pieces, both highly characteristic of the school which shaped and of the genius which gave them birth, and both acknowledged masterpieces of their kind—the Œdipus at Colonus and King Lear. To accomplish this, then, I consider the principal object of this Essay.

We are accustomed to call these two poems tragic dramas. Both words are Greek, and both words properly convey ideas indigenous to Greece.

They are of that class which an undiscerning reverence for the antique has made of universal use. It is of importance that their significations should be rightly ascertained. A drama in its simplest and most comprehensive meaning signifies a fact,—not a fact narrated, but re-called, re-enacted. And the addition of the qualifying tragic superadds an idea of religion, and a reference to a divine purpose fulfilled and discerned in the fact represented. The Œdipus Coloneus, therefore, as a drama of the Attic system, is the representation of an incident wherein the sequence of cause and effect, as designed and directed by Divine Wisdom, is revealed and distinctly marked. For tragedy among the Greeks was, from first to last, a religious institution. The populace assembled to behold it, not as a pastime, but as a solemn rite and mystery belonging to their Bacchic festival. And when the rude hymn of the periods antecedent to Thespis became matured, in the fulness of time, into that superb combination of the lyric and the dramatic, wherein the heterogeneous elements were arranged and united into a musical contrast by the poet's inspiration, no change passed over the sacred and solemn nature of the institution. The rights of religion in it were inalienable; and though the direct worship of Bacchus was merged in a more comprehensive spirit of devotion, which addressed the whole number of the immortals, yet that spirit of devotion lost none of its fervency, and only declined with the drama itself. It was its Helicon.

Similar in origin, although widely different in its subsequent history, was the British drama. Invented by priests, and made subservient in the first instance to the interests of religion, it resembled, though in humbler guise and on a less ambitious scale, the pantomimic representations of the principal events of the Evangelical history, still annually exhibited at Rome during the festival of the Holy Week. But the same great event which decided the political destinies of Great Britain, determined also the course of her dramatic history. The founders of our national theatre, after the accession of Queen Elizabeth, dropped the religious character of the drama, and leaving holy things to a more appropriate sphere, established other principles and a new basis of dramatic art. The Greeks had made their tragic Muse a priestess of religion; the English taught her to minister to their thirst for recreation and love of pastime. The former attracted auditors as suppliants to a shrine, by addressing their respect for religion and their affection for their national deities, and fascinated them by gratifying their love of moral beauty and grace; the latter addressed that fellow-feeling for and sympathy with human nature in the extremity of misfortune and peril, which leads us to hold our breath with a painful interest, while the tale goes round the Christmas fire, of murders committed in the silent night, and of the ghost that scares those who walk the churchyard after dark. The former only is the Tragic Drama, the latter is the Romance.

Yet, although not essentially, the romance is often accidentally tragic. For if the principle of tragedy consist, as we have said, in ideas of religion and of Providence, that principle must almost of necessity enter into any drama in which the catastrophe is either terrible or mournful. Death and the grave are among the most strongly suggestive objects of solemn and religious sentiments that we can conceive. And dreadful or serious incident of this kind is almost indispensable to a production whose principal object is to enchain the sympathies and to fascinate the audience.

The Œdipus Coloneus is essentially a tragic drama. It is the punishment of unnatural sin by supernatural means. If the subject were simply the death of the hero, it would not at once follow that the piece would be a tragedy. But it is a death by the judgment of God, and a judgment mysteriously foretold by the oracle of Apollo, and more mysteriously executed by the agency of the Erinyes.* It has throughout the fearful majesty of a stern religion.

King Lear is accidentally a tragic drama. There is no manifestation of Providence in the death of the sovereign or of his heroic daughter. But the destruction of the three criminals, terribly struck down

* The Furies or destroying Angels of Greek mythology.

in the successful climax of their iniquity, is acknowledged, and represented by the poet, as a dispensation of vengeance. Their death is accomplished, not indeed by miraculous suspension, but by all-wise direction of natural laws. The poet's commentary is:—

> "The gods are just, and of our pleasant vices
> Make instruments to scourge us."

Yet this tremendous incident is not interwoven with the design of the play, nor in any way essential to it. It is rather a point of detail, an unintentional coincidence with the primary law of the Greek drama.

It is then, I hope, obvious that King Lear is not in the strict (*i.e.*, the Greek) sense of the word, a tragedy, although some scenes may accidentally possess a tragic tendency. Upon this principle, then, I intend to proceed; viz., that while the poem of the Greek tragedian is a sacrifice to piety and religious feeling, that of Shakespeare can be considered only as a story told for effect and interest; a study of human nature in extreme anguish and distortion, demanding and extorting a sympathetic impression of pity and terror from all who bear the image or partake the feelings of humanity.

To establish this fundamental proposition was the single object of this introductory chapter. I believe that I shall find it a convenient centre from which to deduce all that I have thought and read upon the proposed subject of the Essay. I purpose now to add a full account of both the plays which we are discussing, in my next two chapters. A fourth chapter will wind up the subject, with a full exposition of such similarities or discrepancies as may be observed in the general design, and in the characters introduced.

CHAPTER II.

FORTUNATELY for our purpose, the story of Œdipus and that of Lear, in their historical, or rather unhistorical, character are very similiar. Both belong to that extensive and pre-eminently poetical class of tales, which, springing up in the earlier ages of national prosperity, are preserved, no one knows how, until they are incorporated without question in the annals of the country.

These romantic and many of them beautiful legends may delight the reader by their individual grace, but they will at the same time offend his eye by the false perspective of their relative position. Stretching back into the most remote periods, they notwithstanding bring us into such proximity with, and familiar knowledge of, the most primitive peoples as contemporary history can rarely attain to. The same roving fancy produced them which created those strange tales of father Jove, his multitudinous amours and his conjugal quarrels. They have long lost credit with the historical, though they continue to delight the poetical, reader. The old British lays, preserved as they have been by the tedious old proser, Geoffrey, though immeasurably inferior to the stately epics of the Greek bards, and many of them extremely dull, are not without redeeming strokes of a more fertile genius; and the legends of Arthur, Merlin, Sabrina, Cymbeline, and Lear, have furnished some of our leading poets with occasional themes.

It is impossible at this distance of time, and in the absence of the earlier poems (those of Pisander and Stesichorus) in which was contained the Œdipodean mythus, to decide how much Sophocles found, and how much he invented. The tale in its original form may in all probability have been something like the following.

In the days when the states of Greece were under the rule of despotic sovereigns, the line of Labdacus reigned over Thebes, and Labdacus was the father of Laius.

Now, the crimes* of Laius had displeased the gods, so that when he besought the Delphic god that he might beget children, Apollo laid a curse upon him, saying, that from the hand of his offspring he should meet his death. So when the child was born, Laius commanded that he should be exposed on Mount Cithæron; but the god watched over the

* Ὦς γὰρ ἔνευσε
Ζεὺς Κρονίδης Πέλοπος στυγεραῖς ἀραῖσι πιθήσας
οὗ φίλον ἥρπασας υἱόν·—Χρησμος δοθεις Λαιῳ.

fulfilment of his predictions. A shepherd found the young Œdipus and carried him to Corinth to King Polybus, and he was brought up at Corinth as the king's son. When he was grown up, being informed by chance of the mystery which hung over his birth, he inquired at Delphi. Then the god revealed to him the decree of the fates, that his father should fall by his hand, and further, that he should be united in unnatural wedlock with his mother. So the affrighted youth returned no more to Corinth, and being led by destiny, took the way to Thebes. And meeting, in a place where three ways met, the Theban king his father, with his train of attendants, and being wantonly attacked by them, he was roused to anger and slew the whole company. On his arrival at Thebes he found the city of Cadmus oppressed by a portentous evil; for the Sphinx, an unnatural and blood-thirsty monster, having the head of a woman, combined with the body and savage nature of a brute beast, haunted the country and destroyed many people. But in those days, ere yet the kingly office was disgraced by tyranny or degraded by unworthiness, a royal nature was not concealed by rags nor lost its superiority when it lost its power. The kingly wisdom of Œdipus vanquished and destroyed the Sphinx, and adding the right of merit to that of descent, he assumed again with superior glory the alienated sceptre of his ancestors. The unwitting parricide receives now with the same unconsciousness the hand of his widowed mother. But the vengeance of the gods tarries not. Withered by the visitation of pestilence, the Theban state is commanded by Apollo to make inquisition for the blood of their former sovereign. The shepherds of Mount Cithæron give conclusive evidence, and the dreadful deeds of Œdipus are brought to light. The miserable queen, thus awakened from her deceitful dream of prosperity, dies by her own hand; and the king himself, after lingering through his remaining years under the torments of the Erinyes, is yet found worthy to fall in battle,* and is buried with funeral honours in the temple of Ceres at Eteon.†

This is the original mythus, to which Homer, in the single mention which he makes of the name of Œdipus, bears indirect testimony. But a younger legend, and one perhaps of Attic origin, recommended itself as possessing many advantages to an

* Ὅς ποτε Θήβασδ' ἦλθε δεδουπότος Οἰδιπόδαο
ἐς τάφον ἔνθα δὲ πάντας ἐνίκα Καδμείωνας.
Il. ψ. 679.

† Lysimachus, quoted by the Scholiast, gives the following detailed account of his funeral:—Οἰδίπου δὲ τελευτήσαντος καὶ τῶν φίλων ἐν Θήβαις θάπτειν αὐτὸν διανοουμένων ἐκώλυον οἱ Θηβαῖοι διὰ τὰς προγεγενημένας ξυμφοράς ὡς ὄντος ἀσεβοῦς. Οἱ δὲ κομίσαντες αὐτὸν ἐς τινα τόπον τῆς Βοιωτίας καλούμενον Κεὸν ἔθαψαν αὐτὸν. Γιγνομένων δὲ τοῖς ἐν τῇ κώμῃ κατοικοῦσιν ἀτυχημάτων τινῶν οἰηθέντες αἰτίαν εἶναι τὴν Οἰδίπου ταφὴν ἐκέλευον τοὺς φίλους ἀναιρεῖν αὐτὸν ἐκ τῆς χώρας. Οἱ δὲ ἀπορούμενοι τοῖς ξυμβαίνουσιν ἀνέλοντες ἐκόμισαν εἰς Ετεωνόν. Βουλόμενοι δὲ λάθρα ταφὴν ποιήσασθαι καταθάπτουσι νυκτὸς ἐν ἱερῷ Δήμητρος ἀγνοήσαντες τὸν τόπον. Καταφανοῦς δε γιγνομένου πέμψαντες οἱ τὸν Ετεωνὸν κατοικοῦντες τὸν θεὸν ἐπηρώτων τί ποιῶσιν. Ὁ δε θεὸς εἶπεν μὴ κινεῖν τὸν ἱκέτην τῆς θεοῦ. Διόπερ αὐτοῦ τέθαπται.

Athenian dramatist. In this version, the unhappy son of the unhappy Laius, self-banished and blinded by his own desperate hand, is said to have wandered into Attica, attended only by his daughter Antigone, and to have expired in some unknown manner in the vicinity of Athens, leaving to the issue of his unhallowed marriage, an awful legacy of quarrels and mutual slaughter, and an overflowing measure of that curse, which had gone forth beyond recall against the haughty, but ill-fated house of the Labdacidæ.

This legend, I have said, would probably be preferred by Sophocles as an Athenian dramatist,—as an Athenian, because it furnished material for a display, highly acceptable, of course, to an Athenian audience, of national sentiment;—as a dramatist, because in it the idea of a Providence, rewarding and retributive, is more impressively developed. For, besides the strictly poetical character of the Œdipus at Colonus, it has patriotic, political, and private aspects highly various and remarkable. But of these I shall have occasion hereafter to speak.

Our poet probably found no more than the vague tradition which connected the fate of Œdipus in some undefined manner with Athens, and consequently with Theseus; the detail and embellishment of the story we may suppose to have been his own. Hippius Colonus, a little deme* to the north-west of the city of Athens, naturally suggested itself as the first resting-place to the journeyer from

* The population of Attica was scattered through upwards of 170 *demes* or hamlets.

Thebes, after his arrival in the city; and the mysterious manner of the ex-king's death, unrelated by tradition, was the foundation of the closing-scene, in which the poet supposes Œdipus to be removed from the society of mortals by the personal interference of the Avengers. All that lies between is merely the necessary working of machinery previously set in motion in the Œdipus Rex. So little of this drama is founded upon tradition, and so meagre the pre-existing foundation upon which it was reared!

To the north-west of Athens, as we have said, and at the distance of ten stadia, is the deme of Colonus, adorned with an equestrian statue of its hero-guardian. There are altars and statues of Neptune and Minerva; and there too is the sacred grove of the Furies, by men uninhabited and untrodden, where the vine, the olive, and the laurel flourish, and the song of the nightingale is heard continually. Hither comes the fallen monarch, a man self-banished and long a wanderer; the young Antigone supports his steps, protecting (frail guardian!) his eyeless old age. They bring with them words of hope from the gods, and oracles promising a term of labours; and even now, though they know it not, a present destiny is leading them onwards towards the completion of its decrees. Wearied, the old man seeks a resting-place within the precincts of the hallowed grove, resigning himself, like a victim on the altar, to the sacrificial knife. In a brief dialogue with a passer-by, he informs himself of the name of that stately city whose marble fanes and gilded turrets are rising into the sky at some distance; is told of the opulence and growing fortune of the Attic metropolis, then reposing in glorious tranquillity beneath the benignant sceptre of Theseus; is warned of his unlawful desecration of the grove, and being informed of the name by which the goddesses, who inhabited it, were known among the people of Attica, recognises therein the fulfilment of an oracle, and breaking forth into passionate supplication, refuses to quit the seat to which he has unconsciously been led. The stranger departs to call in the aid of his fellow-citizens, and then enter the chorus in an ecstacy of lyrical frenzy. An agitating dialogue ensues, in which the name and fortunes of the unhappy intruder, but too well known throughout Greece, are revealed,—a communication which is received at first with religious horror, and then with emotions of pity, by the Athenian citizens, humane as well as pious. Ismene, his other daughter, now enters, bringing new responses from the Delphic god, in which the body of Œdipus is mysteriously connected with the fortune of states, and reporting the near arrival of Creon, reigning king of Thebes, with the purpose of reconducting him to that land which is to be blessed by his presence. The chorus regard with silent sympathy the affectionate meeting of parent and child, and, attentive to the dictates of religion, counsel a peace-offering to the venerable sisters,—a libation of water and honey from the fleece-crowned goblet. Ismene departs upon this errand. Now enters Theseus. We may conceive with what rapturous applause an Athenian audience would greet this genuine emblem of the majesty of their city in that her cloudless day. He receives his illustrious visitor with compassionate respect, and departs, having with prompt generosity extended to him the pledge of his protection.

The action here pauses, and the choral ode mounts. In that sublime strain, by the reading of which Sophocles is said to have confounded the accusers who slandered him for a dotard, they sing thy praise, O sunny plain of Colonus, flower-enamelled, watered by fair streams, fertile of vine and olive, blessed by the favour of sage Pallas and of Morian Jove; thence extending their theme as the exulting spirit swells within them, they recount the glories of the Athenian state, gifted by earth-shaking Neptune with the prancing steed and with the many-oared galley. (We must remember that Colonus was sacred to Neptune.) At the close of the strain Creon enters, having previously seized Ismene while sacrificing unattended to the Erinyes. After an angry dialogue, he carries off Antigone by force, and threatens Œdipus himself. But the turmoil of the conflict reaches Theseus at the altar of Poseidon, and brings him to the succour. Creon is arrested, and the city is roused to the rescue of the kidnapped maidens. The chorus raises a martial strain, predictive of victory; and the reappearance at its close of Theseus in company with the princesses verifies their confident anticipations. But Œdipus is not yet free from quarrels, nor spent with cursing; his son Polynices, now entering, receives in abundant measure the paternal malediction for his criminal ingratitude, and departs to receive its fulfilment in civil war and from a brother's hand.

It is evident that this whole succession of scenes is aimless and useless to the ends of the drama, except indeed to develop the characters of the dramatis personæ, as well as for another object which will be explained hereafter. But now a thunder-peal, sent not without significance from the celestial powers, announces the winding up of the mystery. The hero recognises the signal, and calls for Theseus. Meanwhile the storm increases, and prostrates the soul of the chorus with a pious awe. They pour forth their prayers with incoherent vehemence to the father of gods. Theseus enters, and to him Œdipus gives his dying directions concerning the place of his burial, and enjoins inviolable secrecy respecting it; prophecies the unfading prosperity of Athens while the secret of his resting-place should be preserved sacredly in the line of kings; and finally breaks out into solemn appeals to the goddess of the shades. The two kings leave the stage together.

Then follows a supplicatory ode, and a messenger enters with tidings of the mysterious removal of the wanderer from the eyes of men; he recounts in detail the solemn pomp and circumstance attending his last moments. The wailings of the bereaved daughters conclude the drama.

Sophocles died about 405 B.C., at a period when the loss of the Sicilian armament and the renewed activity of the Peloponnesian commanders had reduced the daring enterprise of the Athenian democracy to a convulsive struggling to retain that liberty which seemed about to slip from its grasp. Then it was that those petty states, which had bowed their heads in abject terror before the sweep of her fierce anger, started up around her in the day of her adversity, eager for revenge and bloodshed. Foremost in the attack and loudest in the bark was Thebes. It is not surprising, therefore, that the patriotic bard, whose name was known and respected all over Greece, should in this, his latest work, have taken advantage of the story of Œdipus to deter the descendants of Cadmus from an impious hostility against the land protected by the bones and the manes of the Theban Œdipus. From the same source sprang, no doubt, that fierce spirit of enmity against the hostile metropolis of Bœotia, which is perpetually flashing and blazing in the Œdipus Coloneus; hence came the mission and defeat of Creon, hence the ascribed virtue in the tomb of Œdipus, which Sophocles, presuming probably on the prophetical powers supposed to form a part of the poetical faculty, has ventured to tack on to the original myth. The prophecy was not inspired, but the poet did not live to be mortified by the failure of his patriotic prognostication. But the charm which was wanting to the ashes of Œdipus seemed to be supplied in those of Sophocles. Through the day of his funeral the enmity of Sparta and Athens slept. Spear and sword kept holiday while the remains of the great poet were committed to the dust.

Besides these more particular political allusions, the character of the work is so distinctly national—presenting such a grand vision of the mythical age of Athens—abounding so remarkably in songs and odes of fatherland—that we may imagine it to have been to Athens, although in an inferior degree, what the Iliad was to Greece in general, what the Æneid was to Rome, and what the Henriade was intended to be to France.

And yet, further, the Œdipus Coloneus abounds in allusions of a more private nature. A story told by Cicero, and repeated in every modern notice of the life of Sophocles, represents the poet to have been deeply injured in his old age by the avarice and ingratitude of his grandsons. Very frequent and sorrowful are the poet's allusions to these misfortunes of his old age, conveyed sometimes in the bitter reproaches of Œdipus, addressed to his ungrateful son, and sometimes in sad reflections upon the decay of affection and faith among men. We may imagine what was passing through the old man's mind, when he composed those noble and melancholy lines:

Ὦ φίλτατ' Αἰγέως παῖ, μόνοις οὐ γίγνεται
θεοῖσι γῆρας, οὐδὲ κατθανεῖν ποτε·
τὰ δ'ἄλλα συγχεῖ πάνθ' ὁ παγκρατὴς χρόνος·
φθίνει μεν ἰσχὺς γῆς, φθίνει δὲ σώματος·
θνήσκει δὲ πίστις, βλαστάνει δ'απιστία.

I have endeavoured in this rapid sketch in some measure to show what appearance the Œdipus Coloneus might be expected to present to an Athenian well versed in the mythology of his country, in the history of Athens, and in the private biography of the poet. No play perhaps owed more, at its first appearance, to those adventitious merits which have other founts than that of Helicon, and which recommend themselves only to contemporaneous critics; at the same time it is but fair to state that no poem could better afford to do without them. In none of his works is Sophocles more exalted in sentiment, or more magnificent in diction; in none is the interest more successfully supported without the artificial machinery of a plot! If in artful management of the fable it be inferior to the Œdipus Rex, or in the living picture of active heroism to the Antigone, yet in its magnificent display of the mysteries of the old Greek mythology it is unequalled. We are there admitted into the solemn groves of that chivalrous and martial Paganism, which surpassed in romantic grace all those immemorial superstitions which vegetated like noxious weeds on the banks of the Nile, the Euphrates, or the Ganges. In the piety of Sophocles there is something far more sincere and reverent than is generally found in the votaries of a refined heathenism like his.

CHAPTER III.

In the remotest periods, long before Britain possessed either authentic history, or even genuine traditions; before Roman ambition, or Saxon tyranny, the rude ferocity of the Dane, or the statelier chivalry of the adventurous Norseman, came to desolate our island; nay, before the massy granites of Stonehenge were piled upon one another by the rude art of those primitive ages, the story of Lear is placed by those monkish chroniclers who recorded, and perhaps invented, it. Sixty years did that unhappily celebrated monarch sway the sceptre of his ancestor, Brute: old age came upon him still in undisturbed prosperity, and he might look forward to a peaceful close of a fortunate and protracted career. But the powers which guide the stars of heaven, and the fortunes of men, had already foretold in the one what they designed to accomplish in the other; and had reserved for the declining years and faculties of Lear, a load of disaster, such as manhood in its vigorous prime could barely have supported. His blasted old age sunk beneath the reiterated strokes, smiting like successive lightnings upon a head enfeebled already by the slower weapon of time, and he presented at length the sad and wondrous spectacle of frenzy following in the wake of dotage, and calamity treading upon the heels of decay.

His story was perhaps as celebrated in the earlier days of our English literature, when it was looked upon with the reverence belonging to an authentic narrative, as ever was that of Œdipus or Priam in the corresponding period of Athenian annals. It was copied by Holingshed from Geoffrey; it was made familiar to the lower classes in the form of a ballad; it was incorporated by Edmund Spenser into the second book of the Faëry Queene. But all these earlier celebrations have faded from remembrance before the magnificent dramatic version in which it has been remoulded by a greater pen even than Spenser's, and compared with which they are but as the grub to the various coloured and bright-winged butterfly.

Geoffrey of Monmouth's narration is a mere nursery tale, destitute of dignity and almost of interest, and in style insufferably tedious and prosaic. Spenser has softened the improbability, but at the same time has weakened the point of his original. He relates it briefly and incidentally, but not without a full measure of that rich elegance and fascinating sweetness of expression by which he is wont to illustrate the meanest theme, and to render the foulest odoriferous. But in none of these narratives could there have been discerned the faintest indication of the importance and transcendent interest which this legend was destined to possess in the estimation of posterity.

Shakespeare has employed a most singular and

original device to overshadow and to conceal the inherent improbability of the tale. He has associated with it another story, almost precisely similar in circumstances,—thereby to preserve the unity of interest,—but more easy of belief, that its juxtaposition may raise the credit of the former incident. We are easily inclined to believe that a royal dotard, unaccustomed to contradiction, might, on slight provocation, disown a daughter whom he loved, when we have seen how easily, and at the same time how plausibly, a powerful intellect, unimpaired by age, may be duped into the same rashness. The misfortune of Gloster leads us to believe in the folly of Lear, which in some degree reflects back the probability it receives. This appears to me to be the obvious explanation of the episode of Gloster, which has been so often censured and so often defended on other grounds.

The opening scene is peculiarly Shakesperian. What Euripides and Æschylus effected by a prologue, Shakespeare commonly employs a few of his subordinate characters to manage in a few lines of introductory dialogue. In a conversation between the earls of Gloster and of Kent, we are informed that the old king, weary of the cares of state, is meditating the division of his kingdom among his three daughters. The intended consorts of the princesses are introduced to us; we learn the situation of Gloster himself, see before us his bastard son, and conceive no very favourable idea of the father who can confess his fault with such easy levity. Then Lear entering in state, formally allots to his two elder daughters their share of the kingdom in solid return for empty professions. The disinheritance of Cordelia follows,—the high-souled girl disdains to buy a kingdom with falsehood; her love is of a kind which dispenses with professions. From this difficult point the poet hastens to draw the attention of the reader by means of the interference and banishment of Kent, Burgundy's rejection, and France's acceptance of Cordelia's hand. We are then carried back to the episode of Gloster; Edmund's daring, unprincipled character is revealed in a short soliloquy; his plot against the character and life of his brother is traced through its first stages. We then return to the court to see the first sparks of discontent flashing out, and the true nature of the professing Goneril displaying its fierce features through the hypocrite's mask. The quick-darting eye of suspicion pierces with ready penetration the thin veil which yet conceals the unnatural treachery, and the whole plot, in all its malignant perfection of detail, bursts at once upon the ex-king's eye, when the time for repentance and the necessity of concealment has passed away.

How pitiable, how hopelessly overwhelming, the condition of the man thus late enlightened! It is as when the felon whose sleep has been full of the memory of past joys which may never return save in the mockery of dreams, awakens to the sudden consciousness of fetters and the dungeon. Thus old Lear, who, in the dreams of his dotage, has cherished enmity for affection, and banished love for hatred; who, in the judicial infatuation which precedes destruction, has poured out the fulness of his love upon the bloodthirsty Goneril, upon the pitiless Regan, and has expelled from his presence the gentle affection of Cordelia and the manly fidelity of Kent; now, for the first time, opens his eyes to the fierce looks and scowling brows which surround him on every side. His heart sickens at the view; he speeds from one enemy to another still more determined, from Goneril to Regan, and from Regan back to Goneril. Repulsed with almost undisguised insult, and with still increasing indignities, driven even from shelter by those who owed to him a kingdom, he hurries forth from the society of men, and there, with the tempest raging above him, and the palace of his relentless daughter behind him, he pours forth that tremendous torrent of mingled sorrow, fury, and despair, which has been always so celebrated among the dramatic portraitures of extreme passion.

By a masterly alternation of scenes, the two parallel plots have been carried to the same point of development, and are here united. By the artifices of Edmund, the fiery duke of Gloster is incensed against his eldest son, who is compelled to take refuge in a precipitate flight from the suspicion and penalty of parricide. In the extremity of peril and indigence he wanders through the country, seeking to disguise his dignity under the appearance of beggary and madness.

> "His face he grimes with filth,
> Blankets his loins; elfs all his hair in knots;
> And with presented nakedness out-faces
> The winds, and persecutions of the sky."

In a wretched hovel, Edgar and Lear, accompanied by the faithful Kent in disguise, and the babbling, wild, but affectionate fool, meet. The feigned lunacy of the unfortunate young hero and the ceaseless chattering of the fool, present a powerful contrast to the more passionate raving of the king. The tempest rages without, and the loud strife of passion and lunacy answers from within, in accents of yet intenser horror. But from this depth of misery Lear is extricated by the interposition of Gloster, and carried to Dover to elude the snares which the savage vigilance of the princesses is still plotting for his life. For this act of loyalty and fidelity Gloster is carried before Regan, and his eyes are put out by her order. But here occurs the first check in the triumphant career of the criminals. Cornwall, husband of Regan, and fully worthy of her, is cut off by his serf, roused to violence by this extremity of outrage. Gloster, blind and beggared, is led by his disguised son to Dover, and there saved, first from suicide by the affectionate artifice of his companion, and afterwards, by his valour, from the violence of his enemies.

At Dover, a French army, accompanied by Queen Cordelia, is found encamped; Albany, Goneril's husband, and Edmund, collect the powers of England to oppose the invading army. Lear is found preaching misanthropy about the fields, and brought into the French camp by the order of the queen; and here occurs a brief lull in the aggravated anguish of the piece. Between two giant waves the tempest-driven boat finds a spot where the hurricane is quiet, and the storm cannot come; even so Lear, hopelessly embosomed in woes that swell and tower on every side, finds a serene interval of profoundest tranquillity where the gale roars aloof. The meeting between Lear and Cordelia has ever been a favourite subject for the painter's pencil. Standing as it does in its lonely beauty amidst the frowns and horrors of this tremendous drama, it shows like the silver-mantled moon beaming out from the murky depth of two seemingly impenetrable clouds.

But the dark masses again roll over its fair face, and the returning night seems yet more fearful from this temporary interruption of its reign. In the battle which succeeds victory remains with the side of England and Edmund. Johnson is at a loss to know why, "contrary," as he says, "to the faith of chronicles," Shakespeare chose to bring this drama to so tragical a conclusion. A different issue to the battle would, as he justly remarks, have set the whole matter to rights, and the curtain would have fallen upon a catastrophe highly satisfactory to his critical code. Such a course was indeed plainly open to the poet, and it remains for us to be thankful that he did not determine upon it. For in truth a happy issue to King Lear would have been as misplaced as an unfortunate issue to "Twelfth Night," or to the "Merchant of Venice." It would have been destructive to the unity of interest. The drama of Lear is of a gloomy and sombre cast; the incidents and the characters strange and portentous. Its sphere is either in the heaven of virtue, or in the very abyss of moral depravity. The iniquity of Edmund, Goneril, Regan, Cornwall, is too pitiless to find pardon; the heroism of Cordelia is too celestial, too surpassingly pure for association with the contaminating influence of baser clay, too elevated to play a part in the universal game of expediency. We should feel ourselves defrauded of our indignation and our tears, should the objects of either remain unpunished or unrelieved. For Lear the aged, the weary-hearted, in the grave alone he is not the object of compassion.

> "O, let him pass! he hates him,
> That would upon the rack of this tough world
> Stretch him out longer."

Lear and Cordelia are made prisoners of war; but vengeance is even now preparing for the oppressors of virtue. Discords in the British camp have been hinted at, and their nature in part unfolded. The two sisters, unaccustomed to curb their violent passions, have each, with characteristic vehemence, set their affections upon Edmund, and therefore their hatred upon each other. The young and politic general deems it imprudent to thwart the wishes of either; and Goneril, ever promptest to dark deeds, has already mingled the poisoned cup for her sister. Edmund, in the moment of his exultation, is cut off,—the fabric of his fortunes bursting like a bubble at the moment of its greatest expansion,—by the hand of Edgar, who impeaches him of treason and vanquishes him in single fight; Regan dies with him, and Goneril closes her desperate career by suicide. Lear, released when too late by the dying repentance of Edmund, appears upon the scene, bearing in his arms the corpse of the gentle and noble heroine, Cordelia, and in the profound agonies of hopeless desolation breathes out his wearied spirit. The curtain falls upon the final triumph of the knightly and chivalrous Edgar, the easy and honourable Albany, the loyal and undaunted Kent.

In a brief sketch like the present, it is impossible to give any but an imperfect idea of a drama so superabundantly profuse of incident as King Lear. Yet I trust it is sufficiently full to convey some impression of the design and character of the piece. Nearly the same period in the life of Shakespeare gave birth to Hamlet, to King Lear, to Timon of Athens. A mind penetrated by the same convictions and pursuing the same trains of thought palpably created all the three. All are bitter and misanthropic in their reflections upon nature and the fortunes of man; all abound in mighty but groaning bursts of dark and melancholy power. In the wild, aimless taunting of Hamlet, in the bitter sallies of Timon, in the lunatic morality of Lear, the poet preserves the same mood, utters the same sentiment:—

> "I am misanthropos, and hate mankind."

We cannot now conjecture the cause of this moroseness, which seems to have been the inspiration of Shakespeare in some of his grandest works. But in none of the many changeful shapes into which the restless and boundless versatility of his genius threw itself did his vast mind gird itself to the strife with such angry majesty, or his imagination assert such sovereign mastery over the whole machine of the passions. His sudden and strange sublimity, his dreary pathos, his conceptions of monstrous iniquity contrasting fearfully with those angel forms which he just displays and then instantly withdraws from the view, form, perhaps, the most remarkable and amazing of his many dramatic moods.

CHAPTER IV.

At the beginning of this Essay I laid down in the briefest manner the general principles of the Greek as contrasted with the British drama. What I simply stated there, the time has arrived to discuss more fully and to determine more accurately.

I explained that the root of Greek tragedy was in religion, and that before Euripides brought forward his incongruous and unsuccessful novelties, no effort of tragic genius was without its theological tendency, and few without their philosophical significance. I contrasted with this the absence of religious ideas and a sacred spirit in the Elizabethan theatre, and I showed how exclusively and essentially it is to be considered a pastime. It becomes my business to develop and apply these general ideas.

In the progress of religious error among heathen nations, the first transition from strict monotheism is to pantheism. This again is corrupted to polytheism. Of the polytheistic age we have a distinct representation in the poems of Homer. But civilization established in Greece brought philosophy in its train, and philosophy effected a partial return to pantheism. The mysteries at Eleusis and elsewhere, as we have every reason to believe, resolved the tales of the cosmogony and the generations of the gods into that allegorical significance which in all probability belonged to their first conception. The universe itself was the god of their worship; and in the sun and the moon, in the ocean and the sky, in the cycle of the revolving year, in the oak of the forest and in the floweret of the vale, in height and depth, in the whole circle of created being, they adored the visible manifestation of the Unseen and the All-pervading. This system of emblem and allegory, travelling back towards the old pantheistic creed, was in its existence and after its extinction a profound secret. But the scanty knowledge of it which we possess leads us strongly to conjecture that we trace something of its nature and tendency in the extant monuments of the tragic literature of Greece. We know that the dramatist, Æschylus, was accused of having in one of his pieces violated the secrecy of the Eleusinian mysteries, and some writers* have gone so far as to suppose a philosophical signification throughout in some of his works. But be this as it may, we cannot doubt that there is throughout the dramatic literature of Attica a more philosophical view of divine things than can be discerned in the Homeric poems, and a disposition to treat the gods rather as ideal abstractions than as positive existences. Thus it is remarkable that Comedy, which in the experience of all nations has asserted the deity of chance and

* See Coleridge's "Essay on the Idea of the Prometheus Vinctus of Æschylus."

taken a practically atheistic view of nature and human life, assuming the existence of man to be aimless and purposeless, made its earliest appearance among the Greeks in close association with the Satyric mythology, that embodiment of the careless and superficial creed which supposes the order of nature to be a mere dance of jovial gods without design or systematic action;—while Tragedy, which, on the contrary, mixes up the idea of God and a Providence in all things, associated itself with the grander and more devotional side of the national mythology, telling dire tales of the relentless rule of destiny, and of the sure though tardy retribution executed on the guilty by the hands of the dread Erinyes or ministers of divine justice. We seem to trace in this spontaneous attraction of the dramatic spirit in its two opposite manifestations of Tragedy and Comedy towards their mythological correspondents, some recognition of the symbolic character and disguised doctrines of the traditional theology of the Greeks. The tendency, which always marks a philosophical spirit, to substitute principles for individuals is moreover conspicuous in the dramatic version of the mythus of Fate. The elder mythologists had imagined three sisters of immortal birth, Clotho and Lachesis and Atropos, who spin and cut with relentless pre-determination the thread of human fortune. But among the tragedians we hear little of "the sisters three, and such branches of learning." The idea has been rarified and intellectualized until it has lost its definiteness and parted with its circumstantiality; a single, half-embodied, grim-visaged idea is left, whom the poets named Destiny.

But before this philosophical process was brought to bear upon the mythological system of their ancestors, Thespis and Susarion had lived and died, and had left to a future Æschylus to develop the idea of a drama. They had related the achievements and sung the praises of Bacchus, as Homer and Hesiod might have done. But when Æschylus began to write the age of philosophy had begun, the Eleusinian mysteries had whispered strange doctrines in the ear of Greece. The mythical odes and narratives of this poet are therefore of far profounder import. They abound in philosophical doctrine and metaphysical theories, conveyed in richly-coloured and sublime allegory. And where the populace was probably content to admire brilliant imagery and golden opulence of fancy, the initiated might, perhaps, applaud in secret the magnificent exposition of moral truth and philosophical theory which presented itself to the eye privileged to decipher the splendid hieroglyphic.

He who studies the Prometheus Vinctus or the Eumenides with this idea will not fail to discover much to confirm it, and though he may not be disposed to carry the doctrine of allegorical interpretation to the length to which some writers have pushed it, he will observe with what evident intention the poet has mingled the symbolical with the real, and what a gorgeous superstructure of philosophical conjecture he has erected upon the slight basis which had been the work of preceding architects.

Now, a polytheism thus philosophized assumes by nature a pantheistic shape. It throws off its grosser sensualities, and mounts upon the wing, like the soul quitting the body, glorified and spiritualized, to the region of ethereal ideas and exalted mysticisms. The ferocious and despotic superstition of India becomes in the philosophical pages of the Vedas a pantheistic code of misty metaphysics. All created things, say they, whether of benignant or pernicious influence, are to be worshipped, because all things partake of the divine nature. This is the latent principle of all superstitious imaginings, whether among Hindoos or Greeks. The Greek philosophizer of the creed of his forefathers regarded each of his multitudinous gods as a member or organ of the great, the universal Being. If the heart is the centre and source of vitality and motion in the human system, so was Jove in the system of the world. If the mind is the guide and directing principle of the human system, though not itself belonging to or connatural with it, so was Destiny in the system of the world. In this way the whole Olympian crew found a solution and an interpretation of their characters and functions. Ceres represented the principle of generation; Apollo, all spiritual impulse;

Bacchus was the god of instinct, whether generous and lofty, as in heroes, or sensual, as in satyrs and drunkards. Hence (be it observed in passing) came his twofold character, the jolly god of wine and the heroic conqueror of India.

From Æschylus dates the introduction of actors representing and imitating the characters necessary to the narrative. Having shown the original design of the drama, as an institution subservient to the religion of Greece, viz., to exhibit the working of the great mundane constitution of which Destiny represented the legislative, and the Olympian divinities the executive, organ, it will be evident with what view men were introduced to speak and act. They are necessary to complete the representation; they represent the objects worked on. Exhibited in this principally passive light, they needed obviously but little depth of characterization. Drawn with a few bold touches, and invested with ideas of nobleness and grandeur such as the might of the Æschylean mind bestowed upon everything it touched, they worthily filled up the picture in which the poet designed to sketch, on a small scale, and within narrow limits, the whole economy of his theoretical Providence.

But with Sophocles came in a new principle, but little known or practised by his ruder predecessors. Their vehicle of attraction had been the sensuous splendour of the spectacle, the dignity of the sentiment, and the brilliancy of diction and imagery. Sophocles was the inventor of the plot. He was the first to discover the fascinating influence of sympathy, and the foundation upon which that sympathy must be built; he perceived the necessity of enlarging the original design in one material point. Æschylus had lightly sketched, and with a careless pencil, the lineaments of humanity; his men are the prey for which the gods quarrel, prizes affixed to the strifes of superior natures; their fate was the vicissitude of a combat in which they had small share, their heroism was resignation, their duty to expect the victor. Sophocles elevated his heroes to a wider and a freer sphere of action; they collect upon themselves the eyes and interest of the audience; the soul of the piece is in the daring independence of their wills. The man of Æschylus is an inanimate mass, helplessly trodden down in the stern discord of principalities and powers, to the might of whose heaven-born sinews his puny strength is as nothing, dragged by turns, like the corpse of Patroclus, from combatant to combatant, until the commanding voice of fate decides the conflict and awards the prize. The man of Sophocles is the living hero, befriended indeed or warred upon by the gods, but no longer their plaything, daring rather, like Diomede, to return blow for blow, nor fearing to shake the spear at celestial armour, and to shed pure ichor from immortal veins.

We may entertain interest for that which has

life and the power of volition, but not for that which is inanimate and at the beck of others, for the free man and for the reluctant captive, though not for the willing slave. We can sympathize with human nature in any shape except that of baseness. The base man, who has lost all self-respect, has no claim upon the respect of others. But with all other forms, whether of exalted virtue or of daring guilt, it is possible, nay, it is natural, to us to sympathize. Independence of character, therefore, must be the foundation of dramatic interest, and this Sophocles saw. But he went further, and added virtue and magnanimity. It was not consonant to the purely religious character of the Greek drama to associate vice and moral impurity or imperfection with that compassionate interest which involves a kind of affection. But to make virtue an object of compassion was difficult to a religion which inculcated the doctrine of rewards and punishments in this life. This dilemma the tragic poets eluded by a somewhat singular device. They distinguished and disjoined the crime of the heart from the crime of the hand, and vindicated the perfect justice of fate, while they excited the compassionate regard of the spectators, by punishing the latter, while they avoided the former. This artificial arrangement may be observed throughout the works of Sophocles, and in some of the later pieces of Æschylus. Witness the unconscious crime of Œdipus and of Dejanira, the pious yet appalling vengeance of Orestes, the heroic disobedience of Antigone.

Let us for a moment survey the idea of Greek tragedy which we have been depicting. Beginning in times when Greek Paganism was a fanciful polytheism, it came into the hands of Æschylus at a period when a race of speculative philosophers had resolved that Paganism, as we believe, into a magnificent though disguised pantheism. This system, we have reason to think, may be traced throughout the Greek drama, which thus became a sublime embodying, animated and endued with poetical reality, of a philosophical theory. The fervid principle of enthusiasm and poetic life which ever burnt and ever rose upwards in the mind of Æschylus, gave it at once the vital warmth and the superb brightness of a celestial birth. Such was tragedy when Sophocles arose. That poet of fine fancy and correct taste introduced a new element of less lofty, but more attractive character. He combined the dignity of mythical conceptions with human sensibilities and sympathies; added to the attractions of a religious ceremonial the indescribable and unaccountable fascination which attends the spectacle of human nature in situations of misfortune and peril. If the Greek drama be compared to the car of Achilles, drawn by twin coursers of immortal breed, it was Sophocles who yoked with them the earthly steed,

ὅς καὶ θνῆτος ἔων ἕπεθ' ἵπποις ἀθανάτοισιν.

If, then, we be asked to state in general terms the design which we may suppose Sophocles to have had before his mind's eye, and to have steadfastly pursued throughout his career as the model of perfect excellence, we answer, that had his life been long enough and his resolution strong enough to have surmounted the prejudices of his age and of national feeling, the goal, when attained, would have proved in principle identical with the romance of Calderon and Shakespeare.

Thitherward pointed all his intellectual tendencies, and thither, had he fallen on better times, he would undoubtedly have been among the foremost to arrive. But a splendid and gay theology, the fountain of all that was sparkling to the eye, damped his intended song, and withheld his fancy and genius from the triumphs they were born to win. His fetters were, indeed, of gold; and an ivy-wreath and an immortality were the fruits of his brilliant slavery. But his vocation was the mastery of the passions; he was created to disturb and to soothe the sensibilities of men; and, like the moon directing the tides, to sit in a higher sphere, with the placid might of a being of higher order, guiding the flux and reflux of emotions which swell below. But fortune shut against him the path whither genius led him: thus much he effected, that human sympathies and feelings should be intermingled, though imperfectly, with that which had belonged only to the supernatural world.

If, then, we are asked to state more particularly the design of Sophocles in the Œdipus at Colonus, we answer that his design was twofold. He chose the subject probably as a mythus powerfully displaying the spirit of the religion of Greece; he found in the progress of the story inducements irresistibly according with his natural impulses to give it the tone of a romantic drama, *i.e.*, of a pathetic and passionate narrative of human suffering and fortitude under calamity. It will require no close examination or protracted inquiry to show this.

That the sacred and theological character may be made palpably manifest at the commencement, the scene is laid in the hallowed grove adjoining the temple of the Eumenides, and beneath the shadow of their awful presence. The fate of Œdipus is a sacrifice consummated on hallowed ground; the Eumenides are the priests; Destiny is the idol on whose altar the victim is laid. All the incidental circumstances, with which the poet interrupts the progress of the plot, reflect light upon this central point. The mission of Creon is not for the living Œdipus, but for his corpse; it anticipates the approaching judgment. After the defeat of his machinations, the tone of the play, which before had had something of triumph in it, becomes strangely mournful. The hour draws nigh; the chorus utters at intervals a wailing note; the thunder-trumpet sounds; the snaky folds embrace their victim; the fearful Presence reveals itself, and Theseus is left standing in stupified amazement by the corpse of his friend, whose spirit the gods have taken to themselves.

This is the religious aspect of the piece, but Sophocles tells the tale not only as a worshipper of the gods, but as a sympathizer with men. The wretchedness of Œdipus, touchingly associated with the heroic virtue of Antigone, and contrasted with the triumphant ingratitude of Polynices, and the relentless cruelty of Creon, divides the spectator's interest with the unseen but not unfelt policies of the gods. Thus religious awe struggles with human pity, and alternately with it takes possession of the mind.

It requires no long inquiry into the history of the British drama to determine the design of the tragedy of King Lear. The poets of the Elizabethan age were shackled by no dominant and oppressive theology, nor compelled to sacrifice the freedom of their inspiration to the force of uncongenial circumstances. They copied natural models as genius taught them. They told the story with that regularity which is engendered by natural emotions, and which can afford to sacrifice that superficial symmetry of form, which is indeed the appropriate characteristic of classical literature.

King Lear is a tale of unnatural sins and monstrous villainies, of warm hearts contending with cold ones, of childish affection matched against calculating and far-reaching malignity, of old age against youth, and fathers against children. It may be summed up in the vigorous words of Gloster:—

> "These late eclipses in the sun and moon portend no good to us: love cools, friendship falls off, brothers divide: in cities, mutinies; in countries, discord; in palaces, treason; and the bond cracked between son and father. This villain of mine comes under the prediction; there's son against father: the king falls from the bias of nature; there's father against child. And the noble and true-hearted Kent banished! his offence, honesty! Strange! strange!"

But Gloster had not seen the half of the strange things growing up around him. He had seen the rash anger of Lear, but he had not seen the glorious heroism of Cordelia; he himself had begun to be involved in the prevailing plague of unnatural divisions, but he had not yet been consoled by the daring virtue and dauntless fidelity of his first-born, Edgar. Sombre and terrific as the story is, it has its brilliant lights as well as its dark shadows, and the beauty of the former is as overpowering as the horror of the latter. It is as though every fresh outpouring of infernal fire were followed by a counteracting flood of heaven's own blessed light, and every new armament of the evil cause were met and turned to flight by a fresh band of the chivalry of virtue.

It remains to contrast the characters introduced in their points of similarity and dissimilarity. From what I have said upon the nature of the Greek drama, the tone of characterization peculiar to the Greek tragedians will be at once gathered. I showed how, in the first age of tragedy, they were represented but as prizes affixed to the combats of the gods, and therefore portrayed with little discrimination or precision. They were always splendid and beautiful, but without individuality; rather idealized representatives of a species of men, than possessing the marks of independent character, which may be in many cases indistinct, and in some imperceptible, but which must always belong to an individual. They resemble the wondrous images which are revealed to the closed eye and the slumbering fancy. Whether represented as virtuous, or as familiar with every species of guilt, they have always a grandeur and a beauty mingled with a certain ideal obscurity which repels sympathy even while it excites admiration. Sophocles indeed reduced this ethereal conception in pursuance of his scheme of uniting the Classical with the Romantic; but if in his hands they fall from heaven, yet it is not in their nature to breath the misty atmosphere of this earth.

> "In their proper motion they ascend
> Up to their native seat; descent and fall
> To them is adverse. Who but felt of late
> With what compulsion and laborious flight
> They sank thus low?"

Their march is still in mid-air. We can neither think of them as human beings, nor yet as beings of another sphere. They are not without the power of exciting our interest and sympathy; nor do they forfeit their mysterious grace. Shakespeare's art of characterization is to that of Sophocles what painting is to music in the power of expressing ideas. Painting transcribes the appearances of nature and life; music creates less lively but more ideal images, visions of remote beauty, but formless and ethereal as the shapes of a dream.

Coleridge has well said that Shakespeare's characters are species individualized. There are qualities and habits which enter in various stages of maturity into the composition of every character. They have names in the vocabulary of every nation, and it requires no profundity to perceive or skill to delineate them. But to imbed these in the rough stratum of an embryo man; to subject them to the refining and modifying and colouring process, by which they become assimilated and combined with the surrounding mass; to cause elements widely diffused and common to a large proportion of the human race to shape themselves to a new appearance, and to assume a new texture from the character into which they interweave themselves, as transplanted flowers change their hues with their soil; in fine, to stamp the species with the individual, *hic labor, hoc opus est.*

Many of Shakespeare's most celebrated characters are created by the undue distention of some particular passion or propensity of a mind by nature powerful and noble. A state of agitation or diseased activity is thus induced in the mental system, which is followed out by the poet through a variety of circumstances gradually aggravating and intensifying the disease, until it either destroys itself by its own violence, or disturbs the reason and unhinges the intellectual power.

Sometimes a mind thus disordered acts upon external circumstances, so as to bring about some terrible catastrophe, with which the play closes. For example, the peculiarity of Hamlet's mind is a propensity to a procrastinating meditativeness, resolving all that is external and tangible into abstract propositions, the "airy nothings" of the mind, and thus destroying all power of resolve and all decision of character. This, associated with a constitutional fearlessness and an ardour approaching to temerity, creates a kind of internal jar, and produces a perpetual capriciousness of conduct, according as his generous instinct or his calculating intellect gains the ascendency. This peculiarity of mental constitution, dexterously accommodated to external circumstances, causes at length a scene of bloodshed such as even that strong-nerved generation seldom witnessed, and which is only surpassed in Titus Andronicus.

These general principles of characterization will probably be of use in enabling us to understand and compare the conceptions of Shakespeare, always profound and striking, with those of Sophocles, attractive in their simplicity and imposing in their religious significance.

The similarity of the incidents in the Œdipus Coloneus and in King Lear is certainly extraordinary, but a similarity purely accidental could hardly hold to any great extent in the characterization. The fool, that eccentric mixture of professional buffoonery, sound wisdom, and affectionate fidelity; the rugged and savage-hearted Cornwall; Kent, one of those honest, loyal, impetuous, outspoken cavaliers, whom the parliamentary wars brought into notice, but whom Shakespeare had no doubt seen and studied at the court of the first James; Goneril and Regan, the one impetuous, the other pitiless and merciless in deeds of villainy; all these are without correspondents in the Sophoclean drama. The paucity of character peculiar to a Greek play compels us to be sparing of examples. We must here limit our remarks to Œdipus, Lear, and Gloster, Edmund and Creon, Antigonè and Cordelia.

Œdipus is a man struck down and overwhelmed, not by misfortune (this was a light weight, and moreover self-inflicted), but by the consciousness of guilt,—a king distinguished for his piety and devotion to the gods, and now oppressed by the consciousness of tremendous crimes. When we are introduced to him in this play he has already borne the load for many years; the frenzied grief which followed the first discovery has long ago settled down into a serene resignation, from which no protraction of suffering can move it. On the throne his haughtiness and irascible temper moved our dislike, but he rises with adversity, and shows himself the Prometheus of a lower region, and a gentler, yet not less patient soul, bearing the chain with triumphant dignity, and presenting to the vulture Grief "a heart not to be changed by space or time."

It is remarkable how carefully Sophocles avoids raising sympathy out of that which is not in itself purely virtuous. Shakespeare takes a course diametrically opposite. Lear's almost incredible weakness, and Gloster's coarse language and shameless sentiments, raise in our minds, before the conclusion of the first scene, unmitigated contempt for the former, and aversion to the latter. Yet what heroes of the ancient or modern theatre are honoured more signally with the compassion and love of the audience? As the character of each is gradually revealed, we begin insensibly to pity in place of despising the weakness of old age in the one, and to pardon rather than condemn what clearly appears a fault of the surface in the other.

Lear is a man whose faculties, decaying with time, have been gradually absorbed and swallowed up in the enjoyment of loving, and the intense craving to be loved in return. This all-mastering passion presses all the faculties and energies of his enfeebled mind into one channel, and hurries him on in its steady and impetuous current. And when the stream that flowed in search of smiling scenery and green vegetation finds nought on either bank but a desert, bleak and bare, waste and unproductive, then it is that the agony of the play commences:

and as each successive discovery of the dissimulation and treachery of those about him forces itself upon his mind, leaving his childish desires all disappointed and unsatisfied, then it is pitiable to see how his aged mind, rudely disturbed from its quiet grave of dotage, yields up again the dead passions of its younger self, and starts into a frenzied and unnatural vigour, like the ghost of what it once was. In his madness he is gifted with an unearthly knowledge; his mental eye seems at once obscured and unscaled; as though, through the twilight of his darkened reason, are revealed strange shapes and bodiless creations walking the earth secure in their invisibility. Thus all the wisdom which the powerful intellects of Œdipus or of Gloster has been able to gather from an experience of unrivalled bitterness, is surpassed by the supernatural penetration of the royal dotard, gifted, as he was, by the inspiration of lunacy.

Such a character as this is not to be sought among the conceptions of any less mighty imagination; it is exclusively Shakespeare's. It belongs to the same class, and stands upon the same unapproached eminence, as Hamlet. Gloster, possessing an idiosyncrasy far less marked than that of Lear, is more nearly allied to the Greek Œdipus. Under misfortunes greater even than those of Lear, he stands, like Œdipus, erect and unshaken. But he differs from the Greek hero in two material points:— First, he has not the same unresisting dignity of passive deportment. The miseries of Œdipus are of divine appointment, the relief pre-determined and predicted by the god. The lot, then, of the mortal is uncomplaining expectance. The miseries of the British hero are such as it behoves a man to struggle against; he has no oracle to look to, save the voice of heaven in his conscience. More than this, the idea of a perfection in human nature, which belonged to the dramatic principles of the Greeks, made no part of the system of Shakespeare. His heroes have the flexibility, the limited resource, which we see in everything that is mortal and transient. Secondly, he has not the same ideal beauty. His features and his language are homely, and it is only the distinction of unequalled calamity which can, in spite of nature, raise him to a situation of majesty.

We cannot observe the same distinction in comparing Cordelia with Antigone. The heroine of Shakespeare is viewed at a distance throughout the play; we seldom approach her, or listen to the unreserved unfolding of her secret soul. She is like a gay vision, hovering as a guardian angel over her suffering father, and suffering, with unobtrusive heroism, a martyrdom in his cause. But we can still discern the same want of perfectness and indomitable moral strength which is as illustriously manifest in Antigone as in Œdipus. With a firmness and fortitude almost masculine, however softened by the delicacy of her address and manner, the Theban maiden, sprung from demigods and impeccable like them, though not, like them, impassive, guides and protects the helpless outcast from land to land, among unexplored solitudes and half-savage nations. Cordelia is far more gentle in her affection, far less daring in her heroism. If she comes to the relief of her father, it is with an army and a French marshal; if she falls a victim to the readiness and eagerness of her succour, it is with the submissive patience of Ismene rather than with the high and haughty magnanimity of Antigone.

Edmund and Creon are placed in a somewhat similar position of the plot. The latter is the messenger sent to obtain possession of the person of Œdipus; the former is the chief of the party which pursues, and succeeds in capturing, Lear. But there is little analogy in their characters. Creon, in Sophocles's conception of the character, is an anomalous personage, who has always a plausible reason to allege for his base acts, while he creates in the reader's mind an unmitigable and immeasurable aversion. Edmund is of a species which Shakespeare was fond of reproducing,—a softened version of Iago and Richard III. Exulting in a powerful intellect, and deliberately abjuring all honourable principle, he entertains the ambition of being, as it were, an evil angel to mankind, of building a sullen supremacy upon the subject necks and down-trodden liberties of his fellow-creatures.

But Edmund is not completely hardened. His dying moments are passed in repentance and attempted reparations of some of the evils which his life has caused.

We might, perhaps, imagine some correspondence between the characters of Edgar and of Theseus. Both are the protectors of wandering misery, and both finally frustrate the designs of the evil cause. But Theseus is not an individual, but rather a stately impersonation of the Athenian state in the heroic age; he is ever associated with the name of Athens, as the eagle with Jupiter, or the owl with Minerva. Edgar is the model of a knight of the middle ages, the mirror of chivalry and heroic virtue, joining splendid talents with a love of enterprise and with a proud sense of honour that sanctifies both. To compare the two would be to confound the ideal with the real, the poetical personification with the dramatic character.

But it is time to bring this Essay to a conclusion. In comparing Sophocles with Shakespeare, I have compared the representative of antiquity with that of chivalry; the representative of a time when the highest excellence was placed in devotion to the gods, with that of an age when knightly honour and heroic valour were the object of pursuit among men. Sophocles, led by his own genius towards the principle of Romance, was shackled by the fetters of an ancestral theology, of old custom, of national feeling. His design, therefore, was to combine and melt into one the Classic and the Romantic drama. Shakespeare, a genius of higher order, and more independent strain, and born in more congenial times, followed the dictates of nature without opposition. Sophocles is the poet of religion and human nature united; Shakespeare, of human nature alone. The works of Sophocles, therefore, are poems of a particular age and form of society, though containing something of the balm which will preserve them when no other memorial shall remain of Greece and its heroes; Shakespeare is the bard of all times, whose works will perish only with the human race itself.

ESSAY II.

ON THE CHARACTER

OF THE

RELIGIOUS BELIEF AND FEELING

WHICH PERVADE THE

TRAGEDY OF KING LEAR.

ILLUSTRATED BY SHORT QUOTATIONS.

BY WILLIAM YOUNG.

ANALYSIS.

CHAPTER I.

Connexion of Religion and Morality with the English Drama before the appearance of Shakespeare.

Origin of the English Drama.—Religion.—The Mysteries gradually give way to the Moralities.—Moralities become secularized.—Reformation and the Study of the Ancient Writers.—Their general effect upon the English Stage.—Disadvantage of the Christian with respect to the Pagan Writers.—State of the English Drama in point of Morality when it passed into the hands of Shakespeare.

CHAPTER II.

The part that Shakespeare took in Exalting and Purifying the English Stage.

The hidden Moral Principle in all his Plays the reason of their Simplicity and Unity.—Shakespeare, a great Philosopher.—The Christian View of Life exhibited in all Shakespeare's Plays.—Shakespeare's occasional Coarseness of Language explained,—more than atoned by the deep under-current of pure Morality.

CHAPTER III.

The Design of Shakespeare in King Lear is to Exhibit and Inculcate Parental and Filial Virtue.

Importance of the Subject.—God the Author of it.—Influence on all future relations.—Youth the time for learning great Lesson of Obedience to Authority.—It is the Type and Foundation of all other Social Relations.—Importance of the Affections.—Youth preeminently the season for forming or correcting them.—This is peculiarly the Office of the Parent.—Shakespeare's selection of such a Subject by itself a proof of pure moral tendency.

CHAPTER IV.

The manner in which Shakespeare proceeds to execute this design.

The Fortunes of Lear and his Family.—Character of Lear.—The Family Bond broken.—Consequences on Lear.—His Crime one of the gravest nature.—Necessity of some signal Punishment.—The Ingratitude of his Children most severe of all Punishments.—Discipline has no salutary effect on Goneril and Regan.—Their Conduct as Wives.—Their respective Punishments.—The Conduct of the Two Sisters contrasted with that of Cordelia.—Moral beauty of Cordelia's Character.—Shakespeare's truthfulness as a Painter of Human Nature.—Cordelia's Death.

CHAPTER V.

Other Religious and Moral Principles taught in this Play beside that which is its chief design.

First. The Freedom and Responsibility of Man.—Christian View of Men as responsible Beings contrasted with Pagan Views. —Importance of this Truth.

Second. Universal Providence of God.—Christian View of Life does not limit the Powers of Deity.—Universality of this Principle a Justification of Shakespeare's putting it into the mouth of a Heathen.

Third. Faithful Representation of Virtue and Vice, and their effects.—Gloster's Misfortunes the Punishment of his old Sin.—Edmund meets the due Punishment of his Crimes.—Virtue and Vice at last disclosed.—Shakespeare always seizes any opportunity that may present itself of exposing particular Vices.—Selfishness.

Fourth. Power of Conscience.—Forms great distinction between Man and brute Creation.—Long before Conscience can be entirely stifled.—Conclusion.

ESSAY II.

ON THE CHARACTER OF THE RELIGIOUS BELIEF AND FEELING WHICH PERVADE THE TRAGEDY OF KING LEAR.

FROM the very earliest periods in the history of civilized man, scenic representations have been considered a valuable agent in the conveyance of moral truth.

Of the two great avenues to the mind, the eye and the ear, the former is more calculated to give striking and vivid, but, at the same time, less particular and minute impressions than the latter. In scenic representations, the capabilities of the eye and the ear are united to produce a vivid and accurate conception of facts or ideas. It was, without doubt, the aptitude of the stage for conveying thought in a lively and impressive manner, that led to its being so universally employed in all nations and ages for the purposes of religion. And it is a remarkable fact, that wherever the drama has risen to excellence, it has been connected in its origin with religion. Such, certainly, was the case with the English drama.

CHAPTER I.

Connexion of Religion and Morality with the English Drama before the appearance of Shakespeare.

The ancient representations, called Mysteries, or Miracle-plays, were introduced into England before the close of the eleventh century. They seem to have derived their origin from the custom that had prevailed from time immemorial in the Roman Catholic Church of exhibiting, during the service, a picture representing the part of scripture then being read, which was designed to supply the place of books to those who were unable to read. By degrees this pictorial exhibition gave way to something more regular. Instead of painted figures, living personages were introduced, who moreover frequently told the story they were personating. These rude representations then, modified and altered from time to time, formed the foundation of what were called the Mysteries or Miracle-plays.

Their design was the conveyance of some scriptural truth or fact, frequently taken from the Mosaic account of the earlier state of the world, the Apocrypha, the life of Christ, &c.; and the play consisted in nothing more than a rude personification of the characters in the holy narrative. The whole piece followed the same order, and, as much as possible, the same words as the sacred text. It is evident that these representations must have been of the very simplest kind, and totally wanting in "proper dramatic action."

By degrees, however, as the taste for theatrical representations increased, more attention was paid to them, and the stage, instead of being regarded merely as a means to an end, became cultivated for its own sake.

The exhibition of these pieces also was taken out of the hands of the priests, who had heretofore had the exclusive management of them. As a necessary consequence, their purely religious character was no longer inviolably preserved; and they were at last united with the profane Mimes or Mummings, which boasted of an origin equally ancient with their own. This union gave birth to a new species, which gradually took the place of the old Mysteries.

These new plays, which were called Moralities, first appeared about the middle of the fifteenth century. The distinguishing feature in them was, that the characters, instead of being historical, as heretofore, were allegorical. The design still was to promote religion, to uphold virtue (it might be under the names of the principal graces, *Justitia, Veritas, Pax*), and in the same way to expose vice, and to represent the general consequences of each. But the *wholly* religious character and tendency were now gone, and one of the chief attractions was created by the introduction, in the most grotesque and fantastic forms, of Vice and the

Devil, who, as Coleridge tells us, were the prototypes of the modern characters of Harlequin and the Clown.

The Mysteries were *solely* religious, in their origin, in their purpose, and, indeed, in everything connected with them. From their very nature they were thoroughly epical.

In the Moralities, on the other hand, the design was still highly religious, but the execution of that design was far more artistic. *Their* object was to draw a representation of ideal excellence, worthy of universal imitation.

Under allegorical garbs, the world of morals was brought forth, and brought down to the understanding of every-day men. The Mysteries were entirely epical, the Moralities were as entirely lyrical. Thus the two great elements of dramatic poetry were at hand. But it was only when these had been properly united and blended, that the drama could be said to have risen to its last and perfect form. To accomplish this union, however, required an interval of more than a century, and a genius no less than that of Shakespeare himself.

The Moralities gradually became more and more secularized in their details, and in the reign of Henry VII. they had all but lost their wholly moral aim. Thus we find one Morality of this period having for its title, "The Necessity of the Study of Philosophy." About this time, too, the practice of introducing characters in real life arose, which perhaps contributed as much as anything to the extension of the domain of the drama. And here I must point out two causes which mightily affected the English Drama.

The first of these was the Reformation, which so completely changed the tone of thinking of that age.

The spirit of the Reformation was liberty. It ridiculed and cast behind it the blind belief in whatever was old (as being such), and taught that whatever is *true*, either in art, or natural philosophy, or morals, or religion, deserves attention and respect, whether it be new, or decked out in the hoary vesture of antiquity.

The effect upon the drama was, that the English writers freely followed their natural bent, untrammelled by laws, which would inevitably have dwarfed and ruined them. As might naturally have been expected, this freedom of the earlier dramatists often degenerated into a wild irregularity, which might have proved extremely hurtful, had not a counteracting cause been at hand to check it.

The second circumstance which exerted a powerful influence on the English stage, was the study of the great masters of antiquity. The great imperfection of the English stage, at the period to which we now refer, was undefinedness of form, and want of order and perspicuity, and also of probable and natural causes for the events of the play. This naturally led to a heaping together of characters and incidents, in order to make up for the interest lost by a want of proper dramatic action. A powerful antidote to these evils was supplied by the study of writers, who perhaps are more distinguished for "finished perfection of form," than for anything else.

While this study could not fetter the force of native genius, it nevertheless inspired profound respect for those rules of art, on which the ancient drama depended.

But in examining the ancient classical models, the Christian dramatist must at once have seen that he stood at a great disadvantage, in certain respects, when compared with the Pagan writer. The Pagan regarded the Deity in an aspect totally different from the Christian. *His* god was altogether objective, palpable, could appear visibly, and take an actual share in the affairs of mortals. Did justice and morality demand a speedy punishment for some extraordinary crime, then either the father of the gods himself, or his immediate messenger, appeared to chastise the glaring impiety. The poet considered it no way degrading to represent Jove himself as visibly interposing, with his avenging thunderbolt, and hurling the impious Phaeton to the lowest Hades, and restoring moral order to the universe.

Again, the mystic heroes of the ancient drama, half divine, half human, were the representatives of universal qualities. Was the object for the while the portrayal of any one of the attributes of human nature, it was easily effected in the peculiar character of the hero introduced.

The Christian God, on the other hand, is unseen, is wholly spiritual; and consequently none of the effects ascribed in the ancient drama simply and naturally to the power of the Deity, could be represented in the same way by the Christian poet.

This circumstance it was, perhaps, more than anything else, that gave rise to the vast and awkward machinery of personages, intrigues, incidents, &c., that are observed in the early English drama.

Again, the want of emblematic representations of the general qualities of human nature had to be compensated by numerous repetitions of it, in different characters, scenes, and conditions, so as to produce the same effect, which the symbolical representation of the quality, in the person of a demi-god, had otherwise done.

Such was, as it were, the exterior condition of the drama when Shakespeare appeared. Was it *at heart* sound and uncorrupted? Truth compels us to confess it was far from being so. The dramatists of that day had no proper notion of the dignity and high aim of their work. Many of the most talented and popular among them were immoral in the extreme. From them nothing high or great, nothing at least pure or ennobling, could be expected. Even the best of them looked upon the drama in scarcely any other light than as a means of affording passing gratification. There was need of a genius who, by his talents, should not only perfect the drama considered as a work of art, but who should also raise it to its true position, as an instrument of instruction to the people. Shakespeare gloriously performed this great work.

CHAPTER II.

The Part that Shakespeare took in Exalting and Purifying the English Stage.

Shakespeare saw that the great defect of his predecessors had been the want of a *deep hidden centre*, around which all the visible exterior of the play should move.

On this subject, Dr. Ulrici, in his Dramatic Art of Shakespeare, says:—

"It has already been frequently observed, and among others by Goethe, that, unlike other poets, Shakespeare did not choose for his several works a particular subject-matter, but that, setting out with a certain idea, he makes this the centre to which he adjusts his materials, and applies for *its* elucidation the world of history and imagination."

It is this fact that distinguishes him from all the dramatists of his country.

However varied his characters and scenes may be, his plays invariably present to the spectator the appearance of a complete and perfect whole, finished in itself. The hidden idea which pervades the whole, like a concealed magnet, draws into and sustains every character in its proper position. His mighty genius reduced the vast chaos to order, and blended the unwieldy masses into a natural and simple union of the epic with the lyric. His catastrophe was the inevitable result to be expected in the natural and ordinary course of events.

More than all, Shakespeare was not only a keen observer and a true poet, but he was a profound philosopher. He had looked upon life from different points of view, and had been enabled to obtain a just and comprehensive idea of it.

He exhibits God as the Moral Governor of the universe, and the Disposer of the effects of the actions of men, but he nevertheless declares that no constraint is put upon them, but that they are left to choose and act for themselves.

This is the general christian view of life that is exhibited by Shakespeare in his plays, the pure stream that flows through them all, enriching and beautifying wherever it goes. This it is that renders Shakespeare's plays valuable, not merely as works of art, but as storehouses of morality and virtue. Shakespeare's language often sounds to our ears coarse and gross; but we should remember that it is not fair to take him out of his age, and compare his diction with that of an age infinitely more refined. The only just way is, to compare him with other writers of his own time, and we shall find such comparison turn out immeasurably to his advantage. But even if this fault were far worse than it is, we should nevertheless feel that it is more than corrected by the great moral current that flows through, sweeping and bearing away all the imperfections that float on the surface. And to continue the analogy, *all* that is reprehensible floats on the surface, and is seen at once. There is no hidden under-current, which, while smooth and pure at the surface, is nevertheless silently bearing away the spectator to unfathomable depths. On the contrary, the tendency of all that is underneath is pure and ennobling.

CHAPTER III.

THE MORAL AIM OF SHAKESPEARE IN THE PLAY OF KING LEAR IS TO EXHIBIT AND INCULCATE PARENTAL AND FILIAL AFFECTION.

I HAVE stated that in all his plays Shakespeare has some deep underlying truth, the illustration of which is his great end. Perhaps in none of his plays is this more strikingly the case than in King Lear.

The object here is to exhibit, in all its different aspects and effects, the relation between parent and child; to show that unless the love of the parent be real and penetrating, the love of the child will be false and unsubstantial; and further, that if the first and highest (because divine) law of our nature be trampled under foot, no other relation of life can be duly observed.

To state it briefly, the great subject of the play is, "Parental and Filial Virtue."

And if we examine the importance of this subject more closely, we shall perceive the greatest wisdom in such a selection.

From its very nature, the relation between child and parent is the most binding and sacred in the world. It is the earliest; it influences us when our hearts are fresh and green, not yet chilled and frozen by contact with a cold world. God himself is the author of it. It seems as if He had planted that sacred feeling in our hearts on purpose to give men a model of the intercourse they ought to have with one another. Every other connexion is conventional, and can be dissolved at pleasure; but the union of parent and child lasts till God himself, who founded it, severs it again.

If this great and primary relation be misunderstood and broken, no other relation of life can be rightly fulfilled. The being that can withstand the strongest and most holy yearnings of his nature, and that when both internally and externally he has been least provoked to such a course, can never be expected to fulfil his duties as a brother, a husband, or a citizen.

Youth is the season when we receive our deepest and most lasting impressions. The mind is then of that plastic nature which can be moulded and shaped into any form we please. If we have *then* learned the lesson of obedience to authority, custom and judgment, and even inclination, will all prevent us from rising up against it *afterwards*. If *in youth* we have learned that hardest of all lessons, to subdue ourselves, we are far less likely to forget it afterwards. But if, on the other hand, we have never learned to respect a father's authority, if we have disregarded paternal counsels and warnings, if we have grown up with false ideas of ourselves and those whom God and nature alike command us to obey, how is it possible that ideas, thus early acquired, can be prolific of any but the most direful consequences? The seed will bear its own fruit, and we shall not only be wanting in duty to those who have failed to instruct us in it, but in no other relation of life shall we ever conduct ourselves aright. We shall make bad relations, bad citizens, bad men.

A right and intelligent understanding and observance of the relation between child and parent is of the highest importance,—

First, because this is the type and foundation of all the other relations; and because,

Secondly, the affections are the great moving spring in all our actions. True, if we have leisure and will to weigh any action in the strict scales of reason, the decision of the heart may be overruled; but how often is it that we have neither leisure nor mind thus to scrutinize the promptings of our heart!

How necessary, then, that this mighty moving principle of our nature be right in its foundation!

Youth is pre-eminently the season for forming and

moulding the affections, and bringing them into the proper and lofty position they ought to fill.

And by what care and love is not the affection of the child drawn out and formed by its parent! The watchful and untiring love of the mother to her infant has been the wonder of all ages, ever since the creation of the world. It would seem that the Creator had deemed it indispensable that the human being, before one other latent faculty was developed, should be fortified by this great defence, before plunging into the cares and sorrows and selfishness that form the ocean of life.

"Out of the heart proceed all manner of evil things" was the witness of the wisest Being that ever trod this earth. The very same cause that renders the affections, rightly governed, one of the strongest and best barriers against evil, makes them, when unsubjected to the restraints of reason and conscience, as fearfully prolific of evil and sin.

And it is to be observed, that not only is youth the best season for developing the affections, when already rightly disposed, but it is also the best period for checking them when bent perniciously. The same pliant quality which renders the young plant capable of being directed into the right form, renders it also all the more easily brought back out of a distorted and unnatural one. Thus, to check the evil passions of his child, forms one peculiar part of the parent's duty.

For this important task no one is or can be

so well fitted as himself. He has watched its mind ever since it had one at all; and knowledge thus early gained in the open hours of childhood is more valuable than any that can be gained at any subsequent period. Strangers, too, would not bear with its failings in the same way in which the deep natural affection of the parent enables him to do. These, and many other reasons, combine to show clearly that the parent is of all men the most fitted for correcting and counteracting any evil tendency in his child.

But if, notwithstanding all this, either from the natural perversity of the child, or any such cause, this great bond is roughly broken or despised, it betokens a heart radically evil, and fit for the commission of almost any crime, if only inducement sufficiently strong can be held forth. Thus, the daughter whose heart is bad enough to injure and ill-treat the father, turns out, if possible, a worse wife than child.

All this, and far more than this, is comprised under the "Relation between Parent and Child." The limits of an essay do not permit me to say more on this subject.

It lies at the basis of all moral good; and Shakespeare has borne witness, in the selection of such a fundamental and all-pervading truth, as well to his deep penetration and acquaintance with human nature, as to his profound wisdom as a moralist.

CHAPTER IV.

The Manner in which Shakespeare Executes his Design in the Play of King Lear.

Some critics have denied that in all the plays of Shakespeare a great moral end can be found. At all events there can be no such doubt in the play of King Lear. In the whole of the plot, frequently in the particular sentiments delivered, there is a most marked and striking reference to the grand truth of which we have just spoken.

Albany, his eyes at last opened to a full perception of his wife's crimes, thus addresses her:—

> "I fear your disposition:
> That nature, which contemns its origin,
> Cannot be border'd certain in itself."—*Act IV. Scene* 1.

It was the sense of her filial impiety, without knowledge of any other crimes, which led him thus bitterly to upbraid her.

We shall now, however, proceed to the particular consideration of the play with reference to the way in which Shakespeare executes his great design in it.

We have, brought before our eyes, Lear and his family, and it is on their fortunes that the moral aim of the play depends. Lear is represented to us as a man of ardent and unrestrained passions. Accustomed to all the deference and servility of absolute sovereignty, he had never put the least constraint on his will, whether for good or for evil. To oppose that will for one instant is, to his mind, nothing less than treason, and merits nothing less than death. Witness the faithful Kent, banished, on pain of death, solely for his honest, self-sacrificing concern for his master's interests. Lear has equally false notions respecting his position as a parent, as he has respecting that of a sovereign. Not content with unlimited power over the outward actions, he aims at nothing less than the same subjection of the inward feelings. Loving unboundedly himself, he demands a like love from his children. He *demands* it, as if the love of the heart could be compelled and constrained. Unwittingly, he shows us much of his character in that single line:—

> "Better thou
> Had'st not been born, than *not to have pleas'd me better.*"

Besides, he altogether misunderstands the nature of that love he yet so eagerly desires.

He takes the outward, idle, and worthless protestations of love for the deep and hidden devotion of the heart. Even in this *his* will must be obeyed; he will judge love according to HIS standard, and of necessity he must take the consequences of his judgment.

And yet the mere wish for this love, which he so urgently yet blindly craves, denotes the imperfection of a warm and noble nature.

"He loved well, but not wisely." His passions

are his moving principle; and as these have never been subjected to reason or conscience, the actions, the habits, the life, must necessarily be lawless and imperfect. His example has its inevitable effect on his children. He had never implanted in them a due reverence for his authority and for his character. He had never properly set himself to the education of their minds.

Even the great natural tie, which might have yet served in some degree to sustain filial duty, was broken through his false estimate of it. He had habitually received flattery and hypocrisy in its place, and rewarded *them* instead of *it*. The great connexion between parent and child was wholly broken. Its nature and its obligations had been totally misunderstood, both by parent and child. Nothing, then, remains but to trace the sure and inevitable consequences to each.

It may be asked, Was not the evil effect of Lear's conduct, in his paternal character, to be expected to prove as detrimental to Cordelia as to her sisters? We answer, *theoretically* it was, but in *point of fact* it did not. Often, in spite of every disadvantage, the soul is yet kept pure and bright; and at last bursts forth from the surrounding gloom, all the fairer through the contrast with the darkness from which it has escaped. Cordelia, in spite of all, escapes contamination; and her virtue appears all the more lovely, contrasted with the moral deformity of her sisters.

To return, however, to the subject, viz., the consequences that inevitably result from the breaking of this great relation—we see them first in Lear; and second, in his children.

With a master's skill, Shakespeare assigns to each the due reward of his crimes. He sees at once the magnitude of the evil, its vast influence over the future and all the different circumstances with which it is connected; and with this enlightened view of the crime he proceeds to adjudge the penalty that is fitting.

One would be disposed to say, at first sight, that the punishment in the case of Lear was totally disproportioned to the fault; so much so, indeed, as to be a positive imperfection, a want of adequate cause for the evolution of the plot. Such, however, as I have above shown, is very far from being the case. Lear's fault was one of the very gravest nature, extending not only over the present, but influencing, to an immense extent, the whole future lives of his offspring, and of every one with whom they were connected. It was fitting that a crime of such sweeping and universal importance should be punished in some most signal manner.

The great root of all Lear's faults was his uncontrolled obedience to the passion of the moment; his arbitrary spirit, which would allow him to obey no rules in his conduct to his children, which would not suffer him to submit to the task of watching and directing them.

The same spirit would lead him to break out now in passionate love, now in despotic and tyrannical anger. He had thus completely lost the respect of his children, who could not fail of seeing their father's fault.

Gon. "The best and soundest of his time hath been but rash; then must we look to receive from his age, not alone the imperfections of long-engrafted condition, but, therewithal, the unruly waywardness that infirm and choleric years bring with them."
Act I. Scene 1.

Respect was entirely gone; and if this be shaken, the relation between child and parent rests on a tottering foundation, and any unusual blast may level it to the ground. He had neglected his children, and *they* are the means used for bringing down punishment on his head.

And how exquisite the pain of such a punishment to such a heart! For, whatever he had been to others, to them he had been generous and loving to a fault. He had even wronged others to benefit them. Upon them he had blindly lavished, in the rich love of his heart, power, wealth, honour, everything. He had stripped himself of all to benefit them, and the sole recompense he asked was gratitude.

Tired of the pomps and empty honours of the world, he endows them with all he possessed, and seeks a quiet place where he may rest his weary head, happy in the love of his children. How bitter, how inexpressibly bitter, must be the anguish that rends the heart of the old king to meet such a return for all his goodness! At first, all his old spirit comes back. His wrath swells high; he rouses all the haughty pride of his heart, and indignantly spurns the shelter of such a roof:—

> "Saddle my horses; call my train together.—
> Degenerate bastard! I'll not trouble thee."—*Act I. Scene* 4.

But when his passion is exhausted, the full force of the overwhelming blow strikes him. How full of bitter, repentful sorrow is that exclamation:—

> "O Lear, Lear, Lear!
> Beat at this gate, that let thy folly in,
> And thy dear judgment out."

And with what terrible truthfulness does he describe the pain:—

> "Sharper than a serpent's tooth to have a thankless child."

There is, however, still one alleviation. "Yet has he left a daughter;" and how he clings to it, as the last hope! But when *here too* he finds that he has been deceived, convulsed nature is almost too weak to bear the mighty shock, and reason, overwhelmed by such vast calamities, is for a time shaken from its throne.

Under, however, the salutary discipline he receives, he learns to see his selfishness while in power, and to think for the interests of others. Formerly, as Regan said,

> "He had but slenderly known himself."

Under his severe trials, he learned at length his

past errors. He perceived that his former love was headstrong and untrue. Thus he is at last brought to own to Cordelia:—

> "I know, you do not love me; for your sisters
> Have, as I do remember, done me wrong:
> *You have some cause*, they have not."—*Act IV. Scene 7.*

When he is at last restored to his senses and this correct view of things, his course is finished, and a welcome death releases him from all his sorrows.

But in the case of Goneril and Regan very different is the result. They had nothing whatever to plead in palliation of their dreadful crime. There was no reason why they should have acted as they did, any more than Cordelia. No; it was nothing but the complete eradication of all moral feeling from their breasts, a perfectly fiendlike wickedness of heart, that could have urged them to the commission of such crimes. They have not the very remotest idea of the duty they owe to their father. Like true hypocrites, they flatter him servilely while he has anything to give them, but no sooner has he bestowed upon them all he possesses, than they show, plainly enough, their true feelings toward him.

> *Gon.* "Idle old man! that still would manage those authorities that he hath given away. Now, by my life, old fools are babes again, and must be us'd with checks as flatteries."

Far from treating him with the respect his years, if not the circumstance of his being their father, would demand, they look upon him as an useless and wearisome encumbrance, and ill-treat and abuse him in every possible way, and at last refuse him the shelter of their roof, and thrust him forth to the mercy of the furious elements. Such is their conduct as children, and, if our hypothesis be true, we may expect the very worst crimes from natures so utterly devoid of moral feeling.

Regan is united to a man dark and ungovernable, like herself, where everything is adapted to bring her worst passions into full play. Her season of hopeful probation is over, and she is introduced into circumstances where we can only expect to see her speedily fall the victim of her sins.

Goneril, on the other hand, is placed in widely different circumstances. Her husband is a man who, though vacillating and indolent, is yet decidedly of good bias. He is, too, tenderly devoted to herself. In short, everything favours the good principle in its struggle with evil. But in vain. It is too late to hope for any real change. There *is* a certain depth in sin, to which if any mind has sunk, it is next to impossible that it should ever recover.

When the moral feelings are so far gone as to permit such a want of filial reverence as these two daughters are represented to exhibit, it indicates a progress in evil, from which it is almost hopeless that they should ever rise. Like as pent up waters, when they have broken down the dam which has hitherto restrained them, roll on the more furiously by reason of the coercion they have experienced, so Goneril, when she has overcome the restraint of her husband's virtue, rushes into still more fearful depths of guilt, and proves decidedly the worse of the two.

For a short time all goes on well, but the calm cannot last. The appearance of Edmund is the commencement of the temptation, and, as was to be expected, it is immediately yielded to by both sisters. No restraint of modesty, of law, or of affection, is regarded; and they set themselves at once to overcome everything that opposes their wishes. The death of Cornwall seems to favour Regan's design, while it urges Goneril to make a bold stroke for the accomplishment of her end, if she ever wishes it to be accomplished at all. Regan, on the other hand, heartlessly banishing every memory of her late husband, is equally bent upon her views. Goneril, at last seeing no other way, determines to break over the last feeble restraint, and adds the murder of her husband to her other crimes. But here Justice, "*tardo pede*," comes up with the offenders. Regan is poisoned by her sister, who fears she may prove a dangerous rival. Thus her heartless, if not immoral, conduct to her husband becomes the ultimate instrument of her punishment. At the same time, Goneril's plot is discovered by Edgar, whom, by marrying Edmund, she was about unjustly to have deprived of his rights. When all her crimes are thus disclosed, and Edmund, the only one on whom she could now rely, meets his just doom, despair and rage take possession of her, and she fills up the long list of her enormities by adding that of self-destruction.

There is yet one aspect in which Shakespeare has exhibited the great truth, which it is the design of the play to inculcate, and in a way much more pleasing than the last; and that is, by contrasting the cruelty of Goneril and Regan with the dutiful conduct of Cordelia. And how perfect in its moral beauty does her character appear! Here Shakespeare has strikingly shown his vast dramatic talents. We have no long and tedious speeches, no prosaic descriptions. She is seldom brought before us at all, and then very cursorily. But in these passing glimpses we see enough to form a distinct conception of her in all her feminine softness and grace. She stands forth, the representative of all that is lovely and virtuous. She has resisted all the pernicious effects of her sisters' example, her father's injudicious and false training, and the natural effects of her position. The good has overcome the evil, and come out untarnished from the conflict. Her perfect truthfulness, her sincerity and genuine affection, are all brought forward in the first scene, and are sustained with equal art throughout. There is, however, as Coleridge remarks, "some little faulty admixture of pride and sullenness in the tone of Cordelia's reply to her father." This, however, is but another proof of Shakespeare's truthfulness as a painter of human nature. A character without a single fault in it would not be true to nature.

It would seem necessary, that in drawing a picture of human virtue, some slight remains of the earthy must still be exhibited, or the picture ceases to be true. And Cordelia's fault is one to which she would be peculiarly liable. Her parent's folly, nay, arbitrary conduct, and the base, cringing fawning of her sisters, are indeed enough to rouse up her indignation and disgust. And yet there is nothing absolutely culpable. The fault (if fault it be) is rather negative than positive. It is rather a coldness, a curtness, not quite suitable from a child to a parent, than any disrespect, much less positive dereliction of duty. But whatever her feelings to her father at the first moment, they are almost immediately softened down afterwards, and all her anxiety is for his comfort and happiness, when she will be no longer present to look after and care for him. The anxiety and pain she feels on leaving her father to her sisters are sufficiently exemplified in her parting speech:—

> "Use well our father:
> To your professed bosoms I commit him:
> But yet, alas! stood I within his grace,
> I would prefer him to a better place.
> So farewell to you both."—*Act I. Scene* 1.

Yet in spite of all her virtues and loveliness,

Cordelia is involved in the same ruin as the rest. And this, as we are taught by daily experience, is the case in real life. So intimately are the good and the bad united in this world, that the punishment, deserved only by the one, frequently falls with equal severity on both. And yet there is a marked and striking difference in the respective fates of the characters of our story. While the grim tyrant, death, is, to the two sisters, the breaking up of all their hopes, a forestalling of future misery, it comes to Cordelia resting in her father's arms, as the release from all troubles and the commencement of uninterrupted moral perfection. Shakespeare, too, thus gives terrible emphasis to a law which, when violated, demands punishment even from those who personally have not broken any of its requirements.

CHAPTER V.

Other Religious and Moral Principles Taught in this Play, besides that which is its Chief Design.

Even if there had been no one great moral aim in King Lear, there yet remains more than enough to prove Shakespeare to have been indeed a *moralist* no less than a *poet*.

The play is full of sentiments of profound

religious significance. These I shall proceed to notice singly, in what seems to me to be the most natural order. Shakespeare teaches evidently the doctrine of—

I. The Freedom and Responsibility of Man.

Edm. "This is the excellent foppery of the world! that, when we are sick in fortune (often the surfeit of our own behaviour), we make guilty of our disasters the sun, the moon, and the stars: as if we were villains by necessity; fools, by heavenly compulsion; knaves, thieves, and treachers, by spherical predominance; drunkards, liars, and adulterers, by an enforced obedience of planetary influence; and all that we are evil in, by a divine thrusting on."—*Act I. Scene* 2.

The christian view of men, as responsible beings, is essentially different from the pagan one. In the ancient view, man is not the guide and chooser of his own steps. He is represented altogether in an objective light. From the instant he opens his eyes to the light of the world, till the moment in which he drops into the abyss of the past, he appears guided and governed by a mysterious and resistless destiny. From this destiny we see him for ever trying madly to escape, and yet for ever vainly.

The more that it is resisted, only the more surely and quickly is destruction brought down.

The effects of such a theology are evident at the first glance. If all the actions of man are the effects of a will superior and acting in opposition to his own, he cannot in justice be held responsible for them. If they are good, he is not to be commended; if they are bad, he is not to be blamed.

One of two results must follow. Either, since the sense of responsibility is removed, the human being will give himself up entirely to the government of his passions, will almost lose the distinction between right and wrong, will finally lower himself from the man into the brute, or else, as the poet says, "*involvet virtute sua*," he will gather himself into himself, will summon up all the affections, powers, and aspirations of his soul; and thus fortified, will struggle to stand firm against the fiercest blasts of the tempest.

But stunted, indeed, must be the stature of a mind that lives by such a philosophy! Poor, indeed, this defence against temptation! It effectually dwarfs the powers of the soul, it shows no other relation between man and man than as fellow-sufferers. It freezes the mental vigour, and leaves the individual at last like the solitary pine spared by the woodman's axe, standing in the forest's gloom. The autumn winds whistle around, and one by one its sear leaves are swept away, till at last it stands bare and desolate, bereft of all.

The christian view of men and life is the direct opposite of this. It declares that there is no force exerted on any man, that he is left to himself to choose good or evil.

It follows, then, directly, that every man must be responsible for his deeds. Thus, in so far, every man might be called "the arbiter of his own fate." It is evident that this truth is one of the most important and fundamental in the whole range of morals. We have it, therefore, brought forward in the very outset, and again at intervals, in the course of the play.

It is taught in the fact that Cordelia, although surrounded by so many temptations, nevertheless preserves her integrity in spite of all.

This freedom of will is dependent neither on time, place, outward circumstances, nor anything else. It is in the power of each to make his election on the great questions of morals.

II. Universal Providence of God.

While the christian doctrine concedes to man the fullest freedom of will that it is possible for him to enjoy in a world of mutations and chances, it does not thereby limit, in the smallest degree, the omnipotent power of the Deity. This freedom of will, it declares, is the gift of God, who yet ordains and disposes for the best all the events of Providence.

> *Alb.* "If that the heavens do not their visible spirits
> Send quickly down to tame these vile offences,
> 'Twill come,
> Humanity must perforce prey on itself,
> Like monsters of the deep."—*Act IV. Scene* 2.

The belief in this superintendence and governing providence which here marks, and in due time brings down punishment upon the transgressor, is innate in the human breast. It is universal, belonging neither to age, race, nor even religion.

Regarding it in this general light, Shakespeare puts the sentiment into the mouth of a heathen.

He describes in remarkably striking language the lawlessness and anarchy that would inevitably result if there were no such providence.

> *Alb.* "This shows you are above,
> You justices, that these our nether crimes
> So speedily can venge!"

The same remark applies here also. As the sentiment is general, and in a certain degree common to all men, such a sentiment (and many of the sentiments of the play are of this general nature) can be put with perfect reason into the mouth of a heathen, even though it may have a far deeper significance than he can be supposed to have intended in uttering it.

III. Faithful Representations of Virtue and Vice, and their Effects.

Here we have a good illustration of the superiority of the drama over all didactic teaching.

The nature of vice, and its inevitable and ruinous effects, might be set forth in language eloquent and thundering as that of Demosthenes, and yet this would not make the tenth part of the impression that this story does. The reason is just this, that the only way to reach a human heart is through human personalities, possessing human thoughts and human affections.

Of Lear and his punishment we have already spoken. There is a peculiar fitness in the punishment of Gloster. Gloster's fault was an unrepented crime, committed long ago. Though it may be long, yet it is seldom that vice, even in this world, escapes wholly unpunished. "His sin at last finds him out;" and he is punished through the instrumentality of that very son, the fruit of his unlawful marriage.

> *Edg.* "The gods are just, and of our pleasant vices
> Make instruments to scourge us:
> The dark and vicious place where thee he got,
> Cost him his eyes."—*Act V. Scene* 3.

All may go on well for a time, but it is a deceitful calm. It is like the earth, which indeed may appear green and verdant, but bears within its bosom the seed of that dire upas tree, which, when sprung up, will ruin everything that grows near it.

Edmund is represented to us as endowed with an intellect keen and penetrating, which sees at once into and rejects the superstitions of the ignorant and credulous around him. We see in him, however, a radical corruption and badness of heart.

Admire his talents as we may, we yet feel no regard for his person, and a thorough detestation of his character. Shakespeare never clothes vice in a pleasing garb, but sets it out in its true colours, loathsome in itself, and ruinous in its consequences. Edmund's very first speech lets us into his penetrating but unscrupulous character.

> "Well then,
> Legitimate Edgar, I must *have your land:*
> Our father's love is to the bastard Edmund,
> As to the legitimate: Fine word,—legitimate!
> Well, my legitimate, if this letter speed,
> And my invention thrive, Edmund the base
> Shall top the legitimate. I grow; I prosper:—
> Now, gods, stand up for bastards!"—*Act I. Scene* 2.

After his diabolical schemes upon his innocent brother and his confiding father meet with success, he aspires to nothing less than the crown itself. Nay, it is almost within his grasp. One final stroke, and then—but his villainy has reached its height. Thus far he has been suffered to go with impunity; farther he may not.

When he fancied himself already at the summit of his wishes, he is arrested by the hand of that brother he had so vilely injured, and meets the death he so richly deserves. He at last learns the lesson that vice, though long unrequited, must, sooner or later, bring down its effects on the head of the offender.

> *Edm.* "Thou hast spoken right, 'tis true;
> The wheel is come full circle; I am here."—*Act V. Scene* 3.

We have the same great moral truth set forth in the fate of the rascally steward. His dastardly love of gain was the immediate cause of his well-merited death. Sin is sin in spite of every meretricious ornament in which it may be decked out; and virtue is great and sterling, despite all the outward circumstances which veil it.

Goneril and Regan, Edmund and Cornwall, high in station, possessed of all the appendages of wealth, birth, beauty, are nevertheless wholly corrupt and bad. For a time Goneril imposed upon her husband, but at last he saw her true character.

When it came out fully, how great his detestation and horror of her in spite of all his former love!

Shakespeare sets fairly before us the evil, spreading, nature of sin. No matter how externally beautiful any object, if at heart corrupted by sin, he exhibits it as most foul and deadly.

Virtue, on the other hand, may for a while be clouded. Cordelia may be an outcast child, spurned away by her father, and received, as it were, "as fortune's alms," by a mere stranger; yet she at last appears in all the piety and love of the child, in all the patience and true dignity of the woman. Kent may be totally hidden for a time, he may change his lofty rank for that of a humble servant. Yet his virtue, and honest, heartfelt devotion to his master, appear only the more noble for the temporary cloud.

Edgar may be compelled to renounce for a time his proper station, and descend into the very lowest depths of outward human misery, and be obliged by the persecutions of vice "to take the basest and poorest shape that ever penury in contempt of man brought near to beast."

But yet at last the good triumph. Edgar, in spite of his manifold outward troubles, yet stands firm, endeavouring to discharge his duties in the station he now occupies. Meanwhile the shadows pass. Virtue has been shown to be able to give support in the veriest extremities of earthly misery. It alone can preserve us untarnished in the still more dangerous season of prosperity.

Edgar emerges from the cloud that has hitherto enveloped him, and stands forth as the avenger of crime and the defender of order. Thus Albany feels that, excepting Kent, Edgar alone is worthy or capable of sustaining the empire.

> *Alb.* "Friends of my soul, you twain
> Rule in this realm, and the gor'd state sustain."—*Act V. Scene* 3.

Under this head it may be well to notice that, wherever it is possible, Shakespeare takes every opportunity to lash with unsparing severity particular vices, and especially the vice of selfishness. For instance:—

> *Glo.* "Here, take this purse, thou whom the heaven's plagues
> Have humbled to all strokes:
> Heavens, deal so still!
> Let the superfluous, and lust-dieted man,
> That slaves your ordinance, that will not see
> Because he doth not feel, feel your power quickly;
> So distribution should undo excess,
> And each man have enough."—*Act IV. Scene* 1.

Shakespeare here sternly rebukes that selfishness that seems innate in the heart of man. There is no vice more widely spread and few more radically injurious. In a certain degree, it is wise and right that we should be anxious and diligent in our own behalf. There is much truth in the old proverb, "God helps those who help themselves." But very different are the feelings and conduct of the greater part of mankind. They seem to make their object not "how they may most wisely and usefully spend their time," but how they may get through life with the least possible trouble and the greatest possible comfort to themselves. On such principles it is not difficult to explain the gross selfishness and utter disregard to the interests of others manifested by such a vast majority of men. This, too, is often more especially the case when, loaded with the gifts of fortune, they have all the greater opportunities of doing good, if so disposed. So rooted is this principle of selfishness in the human breast, that when a man truly learns to pity those whom fortune has not favoured equally with himself, there is strong reason to hope that a great change has been wrought in him, and that his future life will be on far nobler and wider principles.

It shows the importance that Shakespeare attached to this point that he should have mentioned the sentiment of sympathy with our fellow-men, both in the case of Gloster and of Lear, as one of the first indications of a change to the better, of thinking and feeling.

The sentiment is exactly the same in the collateral passage:—

> *Lear.* "Poor naked wretches, wheresoe'er you are,
> That bide the pelting of this pitiless storm,
> How shall your houseless heads, and unfed sides,
> Your loop'd and window'd raggedness, defend you
> From seasons such as these? O, I have ta'en
> Too little care of this! Take physic, pomp;
> Expose thyself to feel what wretches feel;
> That thou may'st shake the superflux to them,
> And show the heavens more just."—*Act III. Scene* 4.

IV. Power of Conscience.

Conscience has been well called, "the voice of God in man." It is conscience, or the power of distinguishing right from wrong, that, even still more than reason itself, makes the great distinction between man and the brute creation.

The wonderful instinct, indeed, of certain of the lower animals is so marvellous, as very closely to approach to intellect. But there is this conscience still that separates eternally the man and the mere animal. And in proof of this we observe that in some of the human race who have almost lost this great distinction (for instance, the wretched inhabitants of Central Africa) the line of demarcation between the man and the brute is so faint as to be almost imperceptible. But in cases where conscience has been resuscitated, in proportion as it has become healthy and vigorous, has the individual been raised in the social scale.

It is long, too, before conscience can be entirely stifled. Ever and anon it *will* break out, and cause itself to be heard above the roar of the tempest, even above the ceaseless clatter of the world. When the tumult has a little subsided, and a moment's quiet snatched from its unending hurry, *then* there darts into the soul the remembrance of the past and it may be half-forgotten evil, and remains, like an uncured wound, ever festering and green. Thus:—

> *Lear.* "Tremble, thou wretch,
> That hast within thee undivulged crimes,
> Unwhipp'd of justice: Hide thee, thou bloody hand;
> Thou perjur'd, and thou simular man of virtue
> Thou art incestuous: Caitiff, to pieces shake,
> That under covert and convenient seeming
> Hast practis'd on man's life!—Close pent-up guilts,
> Rive your concealing continents, and cry
> These dreadful summoners grace."—*Act III. Scene 2.*

Edm. (*Aside.*) "I will persevere in my course of loyalty, though the conflict be sore between that and my blood."—*Act III. Scene* 5.

How true to nature! Conscience is, indeed, hard to be mastered, even in the most depraved and abandoned villains, and they are fain to get some pretext or other, which, though it cannot satisfy, may at least quiet the unwelcome reprover. Edmund tries to justify his horrible crime by persuading himself that in murdering his father he is only acting the part of a *loyal citizen!*

Just so with Goneril and Regan. After their abominable cruelty to their old father, they endeavour by all manner of excuses to persuade themselves that it is owing to his own stubborn self-will, and to no want of filial duty on their part, that he is deprived of a roof under which he may protect his hoary head from the pitiless tempest.

Reg. "This house
Is little; the old man and his people cannot
Be well bestow'd."
Gon. "'Tis his own blame; he hath put
Himself from rest, and must needs taste his folly."—*Act II. Scene* 4.

How perfect a knowledge of the human heart do not these few lines exhibit! How well the great master understood the doublings and shifts by which evil is fain to hide from its votary its loathsome and deadly nature! Well was it for the drama, in an age when licentiousness and vice in every shape were riding rampant, that there was one so able to explain its nature and its powers.

We do not mean to assert that Shakespeare is the best of Religious Teachers.

We have a far higher and purer standard, along with which Shakespeare must not even be named! But it is sufficient that we have shown he is on the side of virtue, that he has a moral end in his plays, and that his influence is very generally favourable to the great cause of Religion.

ESSAY III.

ON THE

TRAGEDY OF KING LEAR;

QUOTING AND ILLUSTRATING SUCH PASSAGES

AS ALLUDE TO

THE USAGES OF THE TIMES IN WHICH SHAKESPEARE LIVED.

BY ERNEST ABRAHAM HART.

ESSAY III.

> "When learning's triumph o'er her barbarous foes
> First reared the stage, immortal Shakespeare rose."

In the history of the world occur periods when the earth seems overspread with a bleak and wintry chill; when the sciences and arts are at a stand; when nothing is added to the great store of the world's knowledge, and men's minds seem covered with a thick veil of intellectual darkness: opposed to such gloomy periods, in strong contrast, stand others, when the sunny light of reason, bursting forth from behind the clouds of ignorance and superstition, diffuses a genial warmth throughout the globe; when great discoveries are made, and works are written, which secure a world-long fame to their authors; when the arts and sciences alike flourish.

Two of these illustrious epochs glitter with especial brilliancy. The one, when Greece was at the climax of her glory, when on the plains of Marathon she had shown herself worthy of her long-boasted liberty and independence; when a complete system of philosophy had for the first time been given to the world; when the glorious triumvirate of the Drama composed their noble works; when Phidias sculptured and when Pericles harangued. The other, when Shakespeare entered the arena of life. This was indeed a memorable period. The gloomy night of what are aptly called "the dark ages," had now disappeared; the printing-press—that faithful assistant in the progress of civilization—was in full operation; mankind began once more to exercise their intellectual powers, and assert their right to think for themselves; and a galaxy of talent shone forth, "such as the world ne'er saw."

It is of this illustrious age that Shakespeare has become the great exponent to all succeeding generations. One section of his works, his historical plays, he has devoted exclusively to relating the history, and portraying the character, feelings, habits, and manners of the English of his own and preceding ages; and these plays must ever be read, by all who rejoice in the name of Englishmen, with the utmost interest, for truer or more vivid pictures are nowhere to be found. But it is not in these alone that we are to look for illustrative notices of the times in which our poet lived; all his works are thickly studded with incidental allusions of the highest interest, and frequently of some historical value. It is here my intention to notice and explain such of these allusions as occur in the tragedy of King Lear.

"These late eclipses of the sun and moon portend no good to us."
Act I. Scene 2.

A firm belief in the influence of the heavenly bodies over the affairs of men is as ancient as it was universal; but it was especially the besetting sin of the middle ages. It was shared alike by the peasant and the sovereign; the former of whom had some excuse for his credulity when he saw a learned impostor, such as the famous Dr. Dee, not only visited and furnished with funds by the strong-minded Queen Elizabeth, but afterwards protected and encouraged by some of the most considerable of the European potentates. Astrology was indeed "the excellent foppery of the age," and well deserved the satire of our poet, whose strength of mind and clearness of intellect enabled him to see and boldly to expose its absurdity, in an age when the belief in it was so firm and general.

"Eclipses of the sun and moon" have always been regarded by the superstitious with especial dread; all mishaps which occurred subsequently to the awful event were referred to the dread influence of this now well-understood phenomenon of nature. Shakespeare again alludes to this superstition in the following passage:—

Othello. "O insupportable: O heavy hour!
Methinks it should be now a *huge eclipse*
Of sun and moon."

To all operations of the moon especially was ascribed in Shakespeare's age great influence over this sublunary sphere. Shakespeare addresses the moon as the "sovereign mistress of true melancholy;" tells us that when "she comes more near to the earth than she was wont," she "makes men mad;" and that, when she is "pale in her anger, rheumatic diseases do abound." He tells us also, through the medium of Hecate, that

> "Upon the corner of the moon
> There hangs a vaporous drop profound,"

of power to compel the obedience of infernal spirits; and that its eclipses, its sanguine colour, and its apparent multiplication, are certain prognostics of disaster.

"To kill hogs, to collect herbs, and to sow seed, when the moon was increasing, was deemed a most essential observance; the bacon was better, the plants more effective, and the crops more abundant, in consequence of this attention."*

We must not, however, be too severe upon the age which fostered these absurd and puerile superstitions, since three centuries, during which science and philosophy have been industriously and successfully cultivated, have not been found sufficient to

* Dr. Drake's "Shakespeare and his Times," vol. ii. p. 385. Edmund's speech, commenting on his father's superstition, will sufficiently show that Shakespeare, in ascribing to the moon power over human affairs, does not speak according to his own conviction, but uses the language of the times.

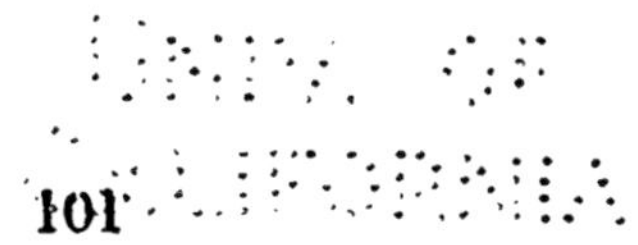

eradicate all traces of them. The doctrine of planetary influence still finds its followers in this country, and that, too, we are given to understand, among the highest classes. Astrological prophetic almanacs still find numerous purchasers;* and Dr. Dee's old trick with the crystal has again been revived within these few last years.

"I do profess to be no less than I seem; to serve him truly, that will put me in trust; . . . . and *to eat no fish*."—*Act I. Scene* 4.

This phrase, "to eat no fish," is a remarkable one; it shows us to what absurd lengths party-feeling will sometimes induce men to go. The explanation of it is this:—In Queen Elizabeth's reign, when the Papists were greatly detested in England, and regarded as enemies of the government, their opponents were carried so far by their dislike to them and their customs, as entirely to abstain from the use of fish, simply because the former party were then, as now, in the habit of frequently consuming it, always eating it on Fridays and other fast days. Thus, "to eat no fish" became the mark of a zealous Protestant and a loyal subject!

This "anti-Papist demonstration" was, however, soon checked by the government; for it was found that if it were allowed to continue, the results would be highly injurious to the fisheries and the

* Witness "Zadkiel's Prophetic Almanac," the author of which boasts of the sale of scores of thousands of his vapid publication.

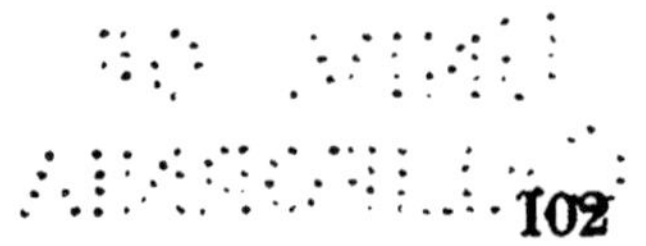

numerous body of persons depending upon them for support. An act was therefore passed to compel all persons to have fish at their tables every Wednesday and Friday, a declaration being appended to the effect that this law proceeded from no superstitious motives, but the anxiety on the part of her Majesty and her ministers, lest permanent injury should be inflicted on the fisheries of Great Britain, or rather England.

An allusion is made to this somewhat whimsical prejudice in Marston's "Dutch Courtezan:"—"I trust that I am none of the wicked that eat fish a Fryday." King also has the following passage, illustrative of this point in his "Vestry:"—

> "On Wednesdays only, fast by parliament,
> And Friday is the proper day for fish."

Mr. Pye, in his Commentary on Shakespeare, informs us that at the table of the king's chaplain, which followed the custom of the old kitchen, fish was for many years only served on Wednesdays and Fridays.

Fool. "Here's my coxcomb."—*Act I. Scene* 4.

The fool in King Lear plays a prominent and well-sustained part, and is employed by the poet as a powerful dramatic agent; we might therefore expect to find in him a character, although taken from life, yet considerably altered to suit the purposes of the drama. This is, however, not the case. Shakespeare has in him presented to us an exact picture of that once indispensable appendage to the household of our ancestors—the domestic fool.

The practice of retaining fools is a very ancient one. "It may be traced," says Mr. Douce, "in very remote times throughout almost all civilized, and even among some barbarous nations." In Shakespeare's time they were to be found in every rank and grade of society; the monarch, the noble, the squire, and even the churchman, had, each and all, their fools: they were to be found alike in the royal palace and the lowly tavern. The materials for a history of them are abundant, and even a close condensation of all that might be gathered relating to them, would occupy far more space than I should be justified in here assigning to it. A general sketch of their manners and habits, including a notice of their more prominent peculiarities, must therefore suffice.

It is not to be supposed that the ordinary run of domestic fools possessed the superabundant wit and readiness of their prototype in King Lear; they were, for the most part, such as the "Innocent," described by Sir Thomas More in his "Utopia," who "so studied his words and sayings, brought forth so out of time and place to make sport and laughter, that *he* was oftener laughed at than his jests were." An excellent idea of their general manners and habits may be obtained from the following account of them given by a writer who was contemporary with our poet:—"Immoderate and disordinate joy become incorporate in the bodie of a jeaster; this fellow in person is comely, in apparell courtly, but in behaviour a very ape and no man; his studie is to coine *bitter jeasts*, or to shew antique motions, or to sing baudie *sonnets and ballads*. Give him a little wine in his head, he is continually flearing and making of mouths; he laughs intemperately at every little occasion, and dances about the house, leaps over tables, outskips men's heads, trips up his companions' heeles, burns sack with a candle, and hath all the feats of a Lord of Misrule in the country: feed him in his humor, you shall have his heart; in meere kindness he will hug you in his armes, kisse you on the cheeke, and rapping out an horrible oth, crie, 'God's soul, Tim, I love you; you know my poore heart—come to my chamber for a pipe of tobacco, there lives not a man in all the world that I more honour.' In these ceremonies you shall know his courting; and it is a special mark of him at the table, he sits and makes faces."*

On the passages in this quotation which I have marked, it will be proper to offer a few remarks. Although the making "bitter jeasts" was one principal employment of the "all licensed fool," it became necessary to take care that this was not carried too far, that the jest was not lost sight of

* Lodge's "Wit's Miserie and the World's Madnesse," 1599, 4to.

in the sarcasm, and that the satire was not too biting. One means of softening down the bitterness of their ridicule was to put on an innocent and burlesque air in the delivery; but they had a more effective method of blunting the edge of their sarcasm, or at least of appearing to do so, in the use of fragments of sonnets and ballads. Of this practice the fool in King Lear affords us a full exemplification. Thus also in an old play, which Dr. Drake asserts to have been published about 1580, entitled, "A Very Merry and Pythie Commedie, called, The Longer thou Livest, the more Foole thou art," we have at the beginning the following stage direction: "Entreth Moros (the fool of the piece), counterfaiting a vaine gesture and foolish countenance, synging the foot of many songs, as fooles were wont."*

It will have been seen from the quotation from Dr. Lodge's "Wit's Miserie," that great liberties were allowed to these hirelings, and that they were admitted to close familiarity with their masters, both of these being absolutely necessary for the free exercise of their buffoonery. They were a privileged class with respect to their wit and satire, but their character did not always protect them, as in the well-known case of the poor fool Archee, who, having offended the Archbishop Laud, was by him persecuted with the most disgraceful severity.

* See Mr. Steevens's Note, King Lear, Act III. Scene 6.

This was, however, an exception to the general treatment of these "innocents." Sir Thomas More* declares, with his usual goodness of heart, that "it is a great reproach to do any of them an injury;" and a similar opinion is expressed by Antony Stafford, in his "Guide of Honour." Olivia, in Twelfth Night, says that "there is no slander in an allowed fool, though he do nothing but rail;" and in As You Like It, the whimsical Jaques exclaims:—

"I must have liberty
Withal, as large a charter as the wind,
To blow on whom I please; for so fools have."†

They do not, however, seem always to have escaped punishment; they were subject to, and occasionally visited with, severe domestic castigation. Thus King Lear, whose kindness to the "poor fool and knave" who follows his master's fortunes is one of the best traits in his character, threatens him with the whip in Act I. Scene 4; and Mr. Douce records several instances of a similar nature, from one of which we find, that when by any instance of intolerably gross licentiousness of speech the fool had offended the ears of modest females, he was treated with great severity.‡ In the latter case the punishment was certainly well merited; but in general I think, with Mr. Douce, that the "chastising

* In his "Utopia," Book II. Chap. 8.

† As You Like It, Act II. Scene 7.

‡ See note to page 506 of the "Illustrations of Shakespeare."

the poor fools seems to have been a very unfair practice."

I had intended to have given an account of the dress, &c., of the domestic fool, but as I have already exceeded the bounds I had placed for myself in writing this article, I must refer the reader to Douce's "Dissertation on the Clowns and Fools of Shakespeare,"* and Strutt's "Dress and Habits of the People of England," where he will find a detailed and very learned description, and must here content myself with the following extract from Minshew's Dictionary, 1627, illustrative and explanatory of the passage with which I head this notice:—"Natural ideots and fools have, and still do, accustome themselves to weare in their cappes cocke's feathers, or a hat with a neck and combe of a cocke on the top, and a bell thereon."

P.S. Still further information with regard to the "Old English Fools and Jesters," including an interesting account of Archibald Armstrong and his jests, will be found in the third and fourth volumes of the "London Magazine," in several articles by the late Mr. Octavius Gilchrist; and many interesting anecdotes will be found collected in Armin's "Nest of Ninnies," and the notes contributed by Mr. Payne Collier and Mr. W. S. Thoms. The introduction to this pamphlet (which is among the publications of the Shakespeare Society) will also be found to contain some interesting remarks, as likewise the reviews of it, contained in the "Athenæum," &c.

* Page 497 of the "Illustrations of Shakespeare." To this dissertation my obligations are numerous; it is the most original and most learned dissertation on this subject anywhere to be found.

"How now, daughter? what makes that *frontlet* on?"
—*Act I. Scene* 4.

The allusion here is to the frontlet which in the sixteenth century formed part of a woman's dress. It was the fashion at this time to wear all sorts of coverings for the face, or "mufflers;" these were of different kinds, sometimes concealing the lower part of the face, sometimes the upper part, and occasionally even the whole face; the first being usually called frontlets, the second chin-cloths: their professed object was to keep off the sun, but they seem frequently to have been used for the purpose of concealing the face; for this purpose the third description seem especially to have been used. This usage gave great offence to the gentlemen, and in Scotland, where it seems to have been more prevalent than in England, it was enacted, in 1457, that "na woman cum to kirk nor mercat with her face mussaled or covered that sche may not be kend." Steevens quotes the following passages in illustration of this practice:—

"Forsooth, women have many lets,
And they be masked in many nets,
As *frontlets*, fillets, partlets, and bracelets,
And their bonnets and their pionets."—*Foure P's.* 1569.

"—— Hoods, frontlets, wires, cauls, curling-irons, perriwigs, bodkins, fillets, hair-laces, ribbons, roles, knotstrings, glasses," &c.
Lilly's Midas, 1592.

"—— And vayle thy face *with frownes as with a frontlet.*"
A Collection of Sonnets, 4to, 1594.

Kent. "This is not altogether fool, my lord."

Fool. "No, 'faith, lords and great men will not let me; if I had *a monopoly* out, they would have part on 't," &c., &c.—*Act I. Scene* 4.

This is a well-merited satire on the numerous and disgraceful monopolies so freely granted in the age of Elizabeth, which were usually obtained by bribing the courtiers to assert their influence, in return for which they frequently received one-half the profits accruing to the monopolist. During the reign of Elizabeth monopolies were granted on almost every article of necessity; and Mr. Hackwell might well declare, as he did in parliament, that "he wondered that bread was not of the number." This prerogative of the crown was abolished by the 31st of James I., and all monopolies, except those for a limited time, were annulled; it was, however, exerted for long after the passing of this act, which was evaded in various ways, and the abuse continued unabated until the conclusion of the rule of the Stuart family. It is alluded to by Decker, in his "Match me in London" (1631), thus:—

"Give him a court-loaf, stop his mouth with a monopoly."

And again, in the "Birth of Merlin" (1622):—

"So foul a monster would be a fair monopoly worth the begging."

"If I had thee in Lipsbury pinfold, I would make thee care for me."—*Act II. Scene* 2.

The allusion contained in these lines is but ill understood. A pinfold is a pound. Thus says

Steevens, in Gascoigne's "Dan Bartholomew of Bathe" (1587),

"In such a pin-folde were his pleasures pent."

Capell asserts, "With certainty, that it was some village or other famed for boxing; that the boxers fought in a ring or enclosed circle, and that this ring was called Lipsbury Pinfold." "But," says Archdeacon Nares, "there is no such place or village."

Steevens attempts to get over the difficulty by supposing that "Lipsbury Pinfold is a cant expression importing the same as Lob's Pound." Other commentators have brought forward various explanations, differing from both those which I have given as being the most pertinent and most probable, but Capell's is, perhaps, after all, the best; and if it should be found that there actually was such a place as Lipsbury, which is really not impossible nor improbable, though all traces of it have disappeared, I should unhesitatingly adopt it, as would, I believe, most others.

"A knave; a rascal, ... a beggarly, *three-suited*, hundred-pound, filthy *worsted-stocking* knave."—*Act II. Scene 2.*

Neither of the two epithets which I have marked would now be used to express contempt, but the usages of society in Shakespeare's time were such as to render them highly offensive. It is to be remembered that the age of Queen Elizabeth was remarkable for the ostentatious finery and absurd love of dress which universally prevailed, and which was encouraged by the queen herself. In the "Gull's Horn-book" (1619), you are informed, that in order to be in the fashion, it is necessary, after having twice or thrice traversed Paul's Walk, to enter an eating-house, and before you return to take your afternoon's walk, "to translate yourself out of your English cloth into a light Turkey grogram." With such fashions as these in vogue, and under the rule of a queen who left behind her a wardrobe of 3,000 dresses, some of them of the most gorgeous description, we can easily understand the reproach implied in the expression "three-suited."

"Worsted-stocking" is an epithet of similar signification, implying meanness and poverty on the part of the person to whom it is applied. From Stubbe's "Anatomie of Abuses" (1595), we learn that although silk stockings were extremely expensive in England at this time, even persons who had not more "than 40*s*. per annum, did not wear them of any other kind."

Silk stockings were not known until the second of Queen Elizabeth's reign, in which year her majesty was presented by her silk-woman, Mrs. Montague, with the first pair ever worn in England. But from Stubbes and other authors we find that they soon became universal, and, in common with all other articles of dress, were carried to a most ridiculous excess of gaudiness. They consisted either of woven silk, or, as it seems, were cut out by the tailor "from silke, velvet, damaske, or other precious stuffe."* The low estimation in which worsted stockings soon came to be held, is evinced by various passages in contemporary writers. Out of those furnished us by Steevens, I select the following illustration:—

"Good parts are no more set by in these times, than a good leg in a *woollen stocking*."—*The Hog hath Lost his Pearl* (1611), *by Taylor*.

We find a similar application of the epithet, "three-suited," to that of our poet here, in Ben Jonson's "Silent Woman:"—

"Wert a pitiful fellow, and hadst nothing but three suits of apparel."

"I'll make a *sop o' the moonshine* of you: Draw, you whoreson cullionly *barbermonger*."—*Act II. Scene* 2.

"Sop o' the moonshine;" probably alluding to some dish current at this time, known by that name. There was a way of dressing eggs called "eggs in moonshine," for which the following is the receipt:—

"——Break them in a dish upon some butter and oyl, melted or cold; strow on them a little salt, and set it on a chafing-dish of coals: make not the yolks too hard, and in the doing cover them and make a sauce for them of an onion cut into round slices and fried in sweet oyl or butter; then put to them verjuyce, grated nutmeg, a little salt, and so serve them."†

Three other methods are subjoined.

* "Anatomie of Abuses," p. 30; and see Drake's "Shakespeare and his Times," vol. ii. p. 105.

† Mayslie's "Cook," p. 437.

Farmer tells us, that in the "Old Shepherd's Kalendar," among the dishes recommended by Prymelyne, one is "egges in moneshine." This dish is alluded to by Howell in a letter to Sir Thomas How:—

> "Could I those whitely stars go nigh,
> Which make the milky way i' th' skie,
> I'd poach them, and as *moonshine* dress,
> To make my Delia a curious mess."

"A sop in the moonshine must have been a tippet in the above mess."*

Such is the generally received explanation of this now obsolete term of reproach. Warburton and Capell adopt a fanciful explanation of the phrase. According to Warburton, it is equivalent to our modern phrase of making "the sun shine through any one;" according to Capell, "this ludicrous phrase imports that he should lay the person he speaks to upon his back on the earth, like a sop in a dripping-pan, for the beams to baste him." Neither of these conjectures will, however, stand for a moment; and though many ingenious explanations have been suggested to me by persons whom I have consulted, that adopted by the elder commentators seems to be by far the best, inasmuch as it has at least some little ground to rest upon, which none of the others have.

A "cullionly barbermonger." "Cullionly" signifies doltish, and is supposed to be derived from the Italian *coglione*. What may be the meaning of the

* Nare's "Glossary;" article "Sop o' the Moonshine." This is the opinion of almost all except Warburton.

term "barbermonger" is by no means well known. Dr. Farmer conjectures, with much appearance of likelihood, that it is intended to convey a reproach against the steward as taking fees of barbers and other tradesmen for a recommendation to the business of the family, and thus acquiring property by mean artifices.

Edgar. "My face I'll grime with filth;
Blanket my loins; *elf all my hair in knots.*"—*Act II. Scene* 3.

This expression, "to elf the hair in knots," is connected with a superstition which prevailed in the middle ages: hair thus knotted being supposed to be the work of elves and fairies in the night, and therefore called "elf-locks" and "elf-knots." Shakespeare again notices this superstition, and another somewhat similar to it in his Romeo and Juliet.

"This is that very Mab,
That plats the manes of horses in the night;
And bakes* the elf-locks in foul sluttish hairs,
Which, once entangled, much misfortune bode."†

Mr. Douce here remarks:—"The line,

'And bakes the elf-locks in foul sluttish hairs,'

seems to be unconnected with the preceding, and to mark a superstition which, as Dr. Warburton has observed, may have originated from the Plica Polonica, supposed to be the work of wicked elves.

* Others, and perhaps better, "*cakes the elf-locks.*"
† Romeo and Juliet, Act I. Scene 4.

. . . . Lodge, in his 'Wit's Miserie' (before mentioned), describing a devil whom he names 'Brawling-Contention,' says, 'his ordinary apparell is a little low-crowned hat, with a fether in it like a fore-horse; his haires are wild and full of *elves locks*, and withy for want of kombing.'"*

"The country gives me proof and precedent
Of Bedlam beggars, who, with roaring voices,
Strike in their numb'd and mortified bare arms
Pins, wooden pricks, nails, sprigs of rosemary."
Act II. Scene 3.

We have here an exact description of a class of beggars now entirely obsolete, but who were very numerous in the fifteenth and sixteenth centuries; and while exciting much compassion from their miserable appearance and semi-insanity, were indirectly the source of considerable annoyance, in consequence of the numerous impostors, who, imitating their wildness of speech and manners and squalor of appearance, went about the country, and, in Edgar's words,

"From low farms,
Poor pelting villages, sheep-cotes and mills,
Sometime with lunatic bans, sometime with prayers,
Enforce their charity."

Decker describes one of these, in his "Bellman of London," thus:—"He sweares he hath been in Bedlam, and will talke frantickely of purpose: you see *pinnes* stuck in sundry places of his naked flesh,

* Douce's "Illustrations," &c., p. 426.

especially in his *armes*, which paine he gladly put himselfe to, only to make you believe he is out of his wits. He calls himselfe by the name of *Poore Tom*, and coming near anybody, cries out, '*Poore Tom is a-cold.*'* Of these Abraham-men some be exceeding merry, and doe nothing but sing songs fashioned out of their owne braines; some will dance, others will doe nothing but either laugh or weepe; others are dogged, and so sullen withal both in loke and speech, that spying but a small company in a house, they boldly and bluntly enter, *compelling* the servants through feare to give them what they demand." It will be observed how closely this account tallies with that of Shakespeare, who has given us a vivid picture of the appearance, customs, &c., of this remarkable race of beggars.

In addition to the artifices here mentioned and those spoken of by Shakespeare, Harrison mentions other means which they possessed of exciting pity: † "As by making of corrosives, and applying the same to the most fleshy part of their bodies, and also laying of ratsbane, spearwort, crowfoot, and such like into their whole members, thereby to raise pitiful and odious sores, and move the hearts of the goers by such places as they lie, to yearn at their

* It will scarcely be necessary to remind the reader that both the soubriquet and the exclamation are used by Edgar in his assumed character, in different parts of the play. The singing songs "fashioned out of his owne braine" will also be recognised as one of his practices.

† Harrison's "Description of England," published with Holinshed's "Chronicle;" Knight's "Shakespeare," vol. i. p. 427.

misery, and thereupon bestow large alms upon them." Thus we have enough of material to enable us to form a pretty correct idea of the habits of the vagabonds who affected the pitiable condition of the real "Bedlam beggars;" and I believe there will be few who will not agree with the author of the "Pictorial History of England," when he says that "the merry England of the days of Elizabeth was, in some respects, a terrible country to live in," if they reflect on the rude state of society which some of the particulars mentioned clearly point out.

The real Bedlam beggars seem to have been much less formidable personages than some of their imitators. "They were," says Mr. Knight, "probably out-pensioners of the hospital, never dangerous, seldom mischievous." In Aubrey's manuscript "History of Wiltshire," which contains, as do all his other works, an unusual amount of accurate and original information, we find the following minute description of this singular and, as it would appear, harmless race of mendicants:—"Till the breaking out of the civil war, Tom o' Bedlams did travel about the country; they had been poor distracted men that had been put into Bedlam, where, recovering some soberness, they were licentiated to go a begging. They had on their left arms an armilla of tin, about four inches long.* They could not get it off; they wore about

* The copy in the Lansdowne collection of MSS., among other various readings, has this passage thus:—"*i.e.*, they had on

their necks *a great horn of an ox* in a string or baudrick, which, when they came to a house for alms, they wind; and *they did put the drink given to them into this horn*, whereto they did put a stopple. Since the wars I do not remember to have seen them." This last particular of the great horn into which the Tom o' Bedlams put their drink serves to explain a passage in Edgar's speech—"Poor Tom, thy horn is dry," (Act III. Scene 6,) which greatly puzzled the elder commentators to explain, as Mr. Steevens's note will sufficiently testify.

The dress of the Bedlam beggars is described by Randle Holme in his "Academy of Armour," who says that he had "a long staff, and a cow or ox-horn by his side; his clothing (is) fantastic and ridiculous, for being a madman, he is madly decked and dressed all over with rubins, feathers, cuttings of cloth, and what not."*

"Poor *Turlygood!* poor Tom!"—*Act II. Scene* 3.

"Turlygood" seems to have been another name for these Bedlam beggars. There was formerly some little doubt about the origin of this word and how it came to be applied in this way, but Mr.

their left arm an armilla, an iron ring for the arm, about four inches long, as printed in some works."—*MS. Lans.* p. 226.

* "Academy of Armour," book iii. chap. 3, p. 161. ("Illustrations," p. 416.)

Douce's very interesting note is, I think, perfectly satisfactory on these points. This very learned and judicious commentator says that "Turlygood" is a corruption of "Turlupin," and that the Turlupins were a wild and fanatical sect that overran France, Italy, and Germany, in the thirteenth century and part of the fourteenth. "Their manners and appearance exhibited the strongest indications of lunacy and distraction. . . . . . Their subsequent appellation of the fraternity of poor men might have been the cause why the wandering rogues called Bedlam beggars, one of whom Edgar personates, assumed and obtained the title of Turlupins or Turlygoods; especially if their mode of asking alms was accompanied by the gesticulations of madmen."*

Fool. "I'll speak a prophecy ere I go."—*Act III. Scene* 2.

Shakespeare seems to have had in all his plays a secondary object in view, independent of the main point of working out his plot successfully. In King Lear his object was evidently to ridicule the leading follies of his age, and more especially its weakness in believing in astrology, demonology, and witchcraft, and expecting the fulfilment of the trivial prophecies which were circulated. We have already seen him, through the mouth of Edmund,

* Douce's "Illustrations," p. 406.

most effectually endeavour to cast ridicule on the so-called science of astrology, and the burlesque prophecy spoken by the fool seems directly to aim at the last absurdity.

Preceding commentators, overlooking the object of the poet in introducing this "heap of nonsense and confusion," have laboriously endeavoured to make sense of it, and Dr. Warburton, by an unwarrantable transposition of the text, has succeeded in some measure in doing so; but Mr. Knight has shown that the intention of the poet is best fulfilled by leaving it in its original condition. I will give this gentleman's very excellent remarks in his own words. Speaking of the theories of Warburton and Capell, he says:—"All this appears to us to pass by the real object of the passage, which by the jumble of ideas, the confusion between manners that existed, and manners that might exist in an improved state of society, was calculated to bring such predictions into ridicule. The conclusion,—

> 'Then comes the time, who lives to see 't,
> That going shall be used with feet,'—

leaves no doubt of this. Nor was the introduction of such a mock prophecy mere idle buffoonery. There can be no question, from the statutes that were directed against these stimulants to popular credulity, that they were considered of importance in Shakespeare's day. Bacon's Essay of Prophecies shows that the philosopher gravely denounced what our poet pleasantly ridiculed. Bacon did not scruple to explain a prophecy of this nature in a way that might disarm public apprehension. 'The trivial prophecy which I heard when I was a child, and Queen Elizabeth was in the flower of her years, was

"When hempe is sponne
England 's done;"

whereby it was generally conceived that after the princes had reigned which had the principal letters of that word hempe (which were Henry, Edward, Mary, Philip, and Elizabeth), England should come to utter confusion, which, thanks be to God, is verified only in the change of name; for that the king's style is now no more of England, but of Britain.' Bacon adds, 'My judgment is that they ought all to be despised, and ought to serve but for winter talk by the fireside: though when I say despised, I mean it as for belief; for otherwise, the spreading or publishing of them is of no sort to be despised, for they have done much mischief, and I see many severe laws made to suppress them.'"

Edgar. "Away! the foul fiend follows me!"—*Act III. Scene* 4.

I have in the preceding note affirmed that Shakespeare had a secondary object in view in the play of King Lear; viz., to throw ridicule on the follies and reprove the vices of his age, instancing the passages in which he has attacked astrology and the pretended prophecies; we shall now see that he has availed himself of the pretended madness of Edgar to assist in exposing the fallacy of the theory that evil spirits took possession of men and tormented them who might be driven out by the exorcisms of the priests: for by making Edgar in his feigned insanity assume the character and use the expressions of a demoniac, he tacitly hints that such was the case with those who were believed really to be possessed by a devil, at the same time that by fastening upon the names of certain devils who figured in a case of pretended exorcism, an account of which had recently been published, exposing in the clearest manner the imposture of the whole affair, he has taken the best possible method of throwing discredit on such a theory, and teaching the people to look upon it with the contempt it merited. The affair alluded to had been recently inquired into and exposed by Dr. Harsnet, afterwards Archbishop of York, in "A Declaration of Egregious Popish Impostures," published in 1603. It was briefly this:—Some Popish priests, desirous of gaining converts in England, set about dispossessing some feigned demoniacs of the devils which possessed them; the farce being played in the family of a Mr. Edmund Peckham, a Roman Catholic. This gross imposture was at length discovered and confessed to by the actors in it. In the confession of Sarah Williams, one of the possessed, a list is given of the names of the devils who infested them, which includes all the most extraordinary and fantastical appellations that surrounding objects suggested or old traditions furnished them with. Among others, we find "Pippin, Philpot, *Mahu*, *Modo*, *Soforce*, *Smolkin*, *Fliberdigibet*, *Fratiretto*," and numerous other gentlemen, whose names impress us with a more favourable opinion of the ingenuity than of the taste of their baptizers.

These names Shakespeare puts into the mouth of Edgar while he is acting in his character of a Bedlamite, in order by this means to throw ridicule on the belief in the existence of devils or evil spirits who possessed human beings. "Peace, Smolkin, peace," could not fail to recall to the minds of the audience the Smolkin of this story; that "the Prince of Darkness" was "a gentleman" called "Modo," and sometimes "Mahu," is told us by Sarah Williams as well as by Edgar; and, as Mr. Hunter remarks, "The foul fiend Flibbertigibbet would lose his veritable existence even in the minds of the most credulous, when it is seen how, in case of merely assumed madness, such names could be used.*"

Thus here also Shakespeare, while employed in carrying out a design conceived in the purest spirit of romantic poetry, and exhibiting the most daring flights of imagination, has consulted the interests of humanity, and has availed himself of the ravings of a pretended madman to combat the superstitions of his time and bring them into ridicule.

* "New Illustrations of the Life, &c., of Shakespeare." By Rev. T. Hunter, F.S.A.

"A serving-man, proud in heart and mind; *that curled my hair; wore gloves in my cap,* ..... *swore as many oaths as I spake words,* and broke them in the sweet face of heaven: . one, that slept in the contriving of lust, and waked to do it. Wine loved I deeply; dice dearly: and in woman, out-paramoured the Turk," &c., &c.—*Act III. Scene* 4.

The list of vices and follies of the fashionable *roué** of the day given us in this passage presents many features of resemblance to those which now disgrace the same class,—vices too generally tolerated, and perhaps even most generally found, in the highest ranks of life, and in classes of society where purity of morals ought above all other qualifications strictly to be demanded from their members. But, notwithstanding this general resemblance, which I believe the vices and follies of the same class in different ages will ever be found to bear to each other, some of the particulars here mentioned being peculiar to the middle ages, seem to require illustration and explanation.

The custom of "wearing gloves in the cap" was a relic of the times of chivalry which still existed under altered conditions in Shakespeare's time. Mr. Steevens tells us, that gloves were worn in the hat "on three distinct occasions; viz., (1) as the favour of a mistress; (2) as the memorial of a friend; and (3) as a mark to be challenged by an enemy. Numerous allusions to this occur in contemporaneous

* It may perhaps be as well here to observe, that the "serving-man" of this passage is not used in the sense of the present day, but in that of a lover,—the devoted "servant" of his mistress.

literature; from those given by the commentators, I will select three, each illustrative of one of these occasions:—

(1) "Thou shalt wear her glove in thy worshipful hat like to a leather broach."—*Decker's Satiromastix.* (Steevens.)

(2) *Hen.* "Here, uncle Exeter, fill this glove with crowns,
And give it to this fellow.—Keep it, fellow;
And wear it for an honour in thy cap."—*King Henry* V.

(3) *Hen.* "Give me any gage of thine, and I will wear it in my bonnet; then, if ever thou darest acknowledge it, I will make it my quarrel."
Williams. "Here's my glove."—*Ibid.* (Theobald.)

With regard to curling the hair, we may observe, that the fashion of dressing the hair was considered by the beaux and belles of these times as an affair of primary importance, with regard to the adornment of their persons. "The gentlemen's hair was worn long and flowing, 'whose length,' says Decker, 'before the rigorous edge of any puritanical pair of scissors should shorten the breadth of a finger, let the three housewifely spinsters of destiny rather curtail the thread of thy life; let it play openly with the lascivious wind, even on the top of your shoulders.'"* It was also fashionable to cherish a long lock of hair under the left ear, called a love-lock. "This love-lock, with its termination in a silken rose, had become so notorious, that Prynne at length wrote an express treatise against it, which he entitled 'The Unloveliness of Love-locks, and Long Womanish Hair,'" 1628.†

* Decker's "Gull's Horn-Book," reprint of 1812, pp. 83, 87; Drake's "Shakespeare and his Times," vol. ii. p. 102.

† *Ibid.* vol. ii. p. 103.

It may not be improper to add, that in Dr. Harsnet's "Declaration," the spirit of pride is said to have manifested itself by compelling the person possessed to curl his hair.

The prevalence of *swearing*, in the age of Shakespeare, was one of its most marked and most disgraceful features. "Oaths," says Dr. Drake, "were unfortunately considered as ornaments of conversation, and adopted by both sexes, in order to give spirit and vivacity to their language; a shocking practice, which seems to have been rendered fashionable by the very reprehensible habit of the queen, whose oaths were neither diminutive nor rare; for it is said that she never spared an oath either in public speech or private conversation when she thought it added energy to either." After this example we need not be surprised when Stubbe tells us, speaking of the great body of the people, that, "If they speake but three or four words, yet they must be interlaced with a bloudie oath or two."

These abominable expletives appear to have formed no small share of the language of compliment, a species of simulation which was carried to an extraordinary height in the days of our poet: thus Marston says—

"—— Marke nothing but his clothes,
His new stampt compliment, *his cannon oathes*,
Mark those."—*Scourge of Villanie*, 1599, book ii. sat. 7.

"This is the foul fiend Flibbertigibbet: he begins at curfew, and walks till the first cock; he gives the web and the pin, squints the eye, and makes the hare-lip; mildews the white wheat, and hurts the poor creature of earth."—*Act III. Scene* 4.

Of the superstition alluded to in the first part of this speech, Shakespeare himself gives us the best explanation in a drama, in which he has introduced many of the superstitions of his age regarding spirits with a most admirable effect; treating them in a philosophical spirit, which, together with the appositeness of their introduction and the excellent language in which they are related, has immortalized them. I allude to the tragedy of Hamlet. Horatio, relating the sudden departure of the ghost when the cock crew, remarks:—

"—— I have heard,
The cock, that is the trumpet to the morn,
Doth with his lofty and shrill-sounding throat
Awake the god of day; and, at his warning,
Whether in sea or fire, in earth or air,
The extravagant and erring spirit hies
To his confine."

Thus also in a hymn composed by St. Ambrose, and supposed formerly to have been used in the Salisbury service, which is quoted by Mr. Douce—

"Preco diei jam sonat
. . . .
. . . .
. . . .
Hoc excitatus Lucifer
Solvit polum caligine
Hoc omnis errorum chorus
Viam nocendi deserit
Gallo canente spes redit," &c.,

the misfortunes here ascribed to the spirit were usually considered to be the operation of witches, who were generally held accountable for all the mishaps of their neighbours; on the other hand, Shakespeare had doubtless authority for attributing these effects to the malevolence of spirits, as he certainly had for accusing the "foul fiend" of leading Edgar "through fire and through flame, through ford and whirlpool, over bog and quagmire;" which was a superstition firmly implanted in the breasts of the vulgar of the age of Shakespeare, the wandering fires which were the means of deluding the unfortunate victim—a benighted traveller or otherwise—being known by the name of Will-o'-Wisp and Jack-o'-Lantern, and believed to be occasioned by demons and malignant spirits. Nor was this belief confined to the common people alone, it was shared in by the educated classes, and we find it acknowledged to be in some degree true in a work written by Lavaterus De Spectris, which was translated into English in 1572 (two years after it was first written), in which, after giving an account of these wandering fires (which modern chemical science teaches us have their origin in decayed vegetable matter), he thus concludes:—"But these things and many suche lyke have their natural causes; *and yet I will not denye, but that many tymes Dyvels delude men in this manner!*" *

* "Shakespeare and his Times," vol. i. p. 400. And this concession, be it remembered, is in a work written for the express purpose of censuring the superstitious credulity which put faith in the wildest legends of supernatural interference.

"Saint Withold footed thrice the wold;
He met the night-mare, and her nine-fold;
Bid her alight,
And her troth plight,
And, aroint thee, witch, aroint thee!"
Act III. Scene 4.

One of the chief of those malignant supernatural beings to whom the gross superstitions of the middle ages, which ever exceeded those of the earliest and most idolatrous ages, had given birth, was the Incubus or Night-mare.* "The Incubus," observes Batman, upon Bartholome, "doth infest and trouble women, and Succubus doth infest men." For the manner in which it molested its victims, I would refer to the quotation as given *in extenso* by Dr. Drake,† and to Mr. Douce's illustration of a passage in Act V. Scene 2, of the Midsummer Night's Dream, where he quotes the following passages from Shakespeare as alluding to this influence:—

Imogen. "To your protection I commend me, gods!
From fairies, and *the tempters of the night*,
Guard me, beseech ye!"—*Cymbeline, Act II. Scene 2.*

Banquo. "Restrain in me the *cursed thoughts* that nature
Gives way to in repose."—*Macbeth.*

To check and counteract these influences, the help of the saints was called in; and invocations to these spells and charms were believed generally to resist

* It may not be unnecessary to observe, that the "night-mare" of the middle ages had no connexion whatever with the equine quadruped so called; the word *mare* being here derived from the Saxon word "mara," an incubus.—See Pye's "Commentary on Shakespeare."

† "Shakespeare and his Times," vol. ii. p. 521.

the efforts of the Incubus, and enabled the person armed with them to shake off the fiend, who is represented as riding upon its victim. The word night-mare we still retain, but its signification is now altered; and the disgusting superstition connected with it, the offspring of that intellectual and moral darkness which the Popish domination in Europe had fostered for many ages before that in which Shakespeare wrote, has fled before the light of reason and religion.

The rhyme which Edgar repeats is one of the spells against night-mare which I have above mentioned, and only differs in substance from some others found elsewhere, in that it assigns to Saint Withold the power of subduing the "Incubus;" this part of the subject has, however, been fully explored by the commentators, and it will not be necessary for me to enlarge upon it. One point, however, seems worthy of notice, which I do not remember ever to have seen remarked upon. Edgar, after reciting the spell against the "Incubus," which was a spirit, concludes thus:—

> "Aroint thee, *witch*, aroint thee!"

Now it has never occurred to any of the gentlemen employed in explaining and illustrating this passage to inquire into the propriety of here introducing this exclamation, though it would certainly seem at first to be somewhat out of place at the conclusion of a spell against a spirit which the Incubus was believed to be; it will, however, admit of a very satisfactory explanation. It is, as I think, to be explained thus: —Scot, in his "Discoverie of Witchcraft," gives us a remarkably succinct enumeration of the feats which witches were supposed to be capable of performing; and among those which were said to be done by the worst description of witches, we find this:—"Some write that they can plaie the part of *Succubus* and transform themselves to *Incubus*."* The adaptation of this extract is, I think, sufficiently obvious. I conceive, therefore, that by the addition of this line the spell is made to include not only the Incubus itself, but the witch assuming, or as Scot has it, "playing the part of the Incubus." Should, then, my explanation be adopted, this rhyme will be seen to allude to another superstition connected with that of the Incubus or night-mare, not noticed by the commentators; and it is this which has induced me to introduce here what might else be considered irrelevant matter.

"Whipped from tything to tything, and stocked, punished, and imprisoned."—*Act III. Scene 4.*

In this place Shakespeare, with the kindliness of feeling which invariably characterizes him, endeavours to impress us with the cruelty of the laws which were in that age mercilessly but vainly enforced for the suppression of mendicancy. The

* "Discoverie of Witchcraft," book i. chap. 4.

severity of the previous laws may be judged of, when it is remembered that these were modified in the cruelty of the penalties attached to the infringing of them by the statutes 39th of Elizabeth and 1st of James I., which directed that the "rogue, vagabond, or sturdy beggar" was to be "stripped naked from the middle upwards, and to be whipped until his body was bloody, and to be sent from parish to parish the next straight way to the place of his birth." Harrison has described the state of the law previous to the passing of these acts with much clearness and simplicity, but in a spirit widely different from that with which Shakespeare has viewed the cruel working of the laws relating to mendicancy. The whole extract, which is one of much interest, will be found in Mr. Knight's notes on this passage. The punishment for "their idle rogueing about the country" was originally, that for the first offence they should "be grievously whipped, and burned through the gristle of the right ear with a hot iron of the compass of an inch about," unless some honest person of substance would undertake under a certain penalty to retain the convicted person in his service for one whole year; and whosoever was a second time convicted, was (unless released as above) to be treated as before, and again set to service for a year; which, if he forsook once more before the year expired, he was to suffer death as a felon without benefit of clergy or sanctuary.

Edgar. "Come o'er the bourn, Bessy, to me."—*Act* III. *Scene* 6.

The propriety of putting this fragment of a song into the mouth of Edgar was, I believe, first noticed by Mr. Malone, who informs us that "Bessy and Poor Tom usually travelled together." The author of "Conscience, or Dick Whipper's Sessions," 1607, describing beggars, idle rogues, and counterfeit madmen, thus speaks of these associates:—

"Another sort there is among you: they
Do rage with furie as if they were so frantique
They knew not what they did, but every day
Make sport with stick and flowers like an antique.
One calls herself poor Besse, the other Tom."

An old woman who was called Bessy* was introduced in the festivities formerly customary on Plough-Monday (the first Monday after Twelfth-day).

Lear. "That fellow handles his bow like a crow-keeper: draw me a clothier's yard. . . . . O, well-flown, bird!—i' the clout, i' the clout: hewgh!—Give the word."—*Act IV. Scene* 6.

Lear here raves of archery, an amusement much in vogue during the reign of Elizabeth; I say an amusement, for the long bow had become obsolete as a weapon of warfare, notwithstanding various efforts to prevent its falling into disuse. It is yet practised by some few persons, but it is very far from being so popular now as it then was. It will not be needful to enter into particulars here concerning the practice of archery, but a few observations

* Stubbe's "Sports and Pastimes of the People of England."

regarding the "crow-keeper," and the length of the shaft employed by the English archers, may not be thought superfluous.

The "crow-keeper" was a man armed with a bow and arrow set up to frighten the crows from the fruit and corn, or in other words, a living "scare-crow." "The 'crow-keeper,'" says Dr. Johnson, "was so common in the author's time, that it is one of the few peculiarities mentioned by Ortelius in his description of our island." So in Drayton's "Forty-Eighth Idea:"—

"And when corn's sown or grown into the ear,
Practice thy quiver and turn *crow-keeper*."

Thus much to identify the character of a crow-keeper; to explain the comparison, Mr. Douce has called in the assistance of the venerable Ascham, who in his "Toxophilus," speaking of *awkward* shooters, says, "Another coweth downe, and layeth out his buttockes, as though hee should *shoote at crows*."

With regard to the "clothier's yard," that is, the cloth-yard arrow here spoken of, I take the liberty of quoting the following excellent note by Sir Walter Scott on a line in "Marmion"—

"The cloth-yard arrows flew like hail,"

which will render any further comment on my part quite unnecessary:—"In some of the counties of England distinguished for archery, shafts of this extraordinary length were actually used. Thus at the battle of Blackheath, between the troops of Henry VII. and the Cornish insurgents, in 1496, the bridge of Dartford was defended by a picked band of archers from the insurgent army, 'whose arrows,' says Hollinshed, 'were in length a full cloth-yard.' The Scotch, according to Ascham, had a proverb, that every English archer carried under his belt twenty-four Scots, in allusion to his bundle of unerring shafts."

So in the ancient and beautiful ballad of Chevy Chase:—

> "An arrow of a *cloth-yard* long
> Up to the head drew he."

"Change places; and, handy-dandy, which is the justice, which is the thief?"—*Act IV. Scene* 6.

"Handy-dandy," says Malone, who seems to have explained this passage better than any previous commentator, "is, I believe, a play *among children*, in which something is shaken between two hands, and then a guess is made in which hand it is retained. See Florio's 'Italian Dictionary,' 1598: 'Bazzichiare, to shake between two hands, to play handy-dandy.'" Mr. Douce quotes the following passage from "A Free Discourse Touching the Manners of the Times," MS.:—"They hold safe your children's patrimony, and play with your majesty as *men* play with children at *handye-dandye, which hand will you have?*" Mr. Douce considers that this quotation confirms Mr. Malone's explanation, which to a certain extent it unquestionably does; but with all due submission to both these authorities, I think that, were the discussion worth entering into, it might be easily shown from this very passage, that Mr. Malone's explanation is probably in some respects incorrect.

"It were a delicate stratagem, to shoe
A troop of horse with felt; I'll put it in proof;
And when I have stolen upon these sons-in-law,
Then, kill, kill, kill, kill, kill, kill."—*Act IV. Scene* 6.

Shoeing horses with felt seems occasionally to have been practised in Shakespeare's age; and an instance of it is recorded by Lord Herbert of Cherbury, in his "Life of King Henry the Eighth," p. 41, where he tells us of a joust "held in an extraordinary manner; the place being a fore-room raised high from the ground by many steps, and paved with black square stones like marble; while the horses, to prevent sliding, were shod with felt or flocks." Other passages are adduced by the commentators which tend to show that the idea was by no means a novel one, either with regard to horse or man, having been occasionally put in practice with respect to both.

During the Hussite war in Germany also, this "delicate stratagem" of King Lear was, I believe, fully carried out, the Hussites shoeing parties of horse and men with felt, and thus stealing upon their enemies and taking them by surprise.

"Kill, kill!" was formerly the word given in the English army, when an onset was made on the enemy. Thus, in the "Mirour for Magistrates," 1610:—

> "Our Englishmen came boldly forth at night,
> Crying St. George, Salisbury, kill, kill!"

So in Venus and Adonis:—

> "And in a peaceful hour doth cry kill, kill."*

> "——To watch (poor perdu!)
> With this thin helm."—*Act IV. Scene 7.*

The "perdu," or "enfant perdu," of the middle ages seems to have differed somewhat from the "forlorn hope" of modern times, although not very widely. The "enfant perdu" was a brave man, or as Polemon has it, "a man of great forwardness," who, wishing to distinguish himself, volunteered for "all perilous and harde pieces of service:" a permanent band of these was formed, to which was intrusted the carrying out of all difficult enterprises; it is this permanence which constituted one of the principal distinctions between the forlorn hope and the enfants perdus. To the members of this band it was "lawfull by reason of the prerogative of their prowesse, to beare an ensigne, to have conducte and double wages all their life long."† The institution

* Malone's Notes to King Lear, Act IV. Scene 6.

† Polemon's "Collection of Battels," 4to, Book I. Also see Notes by Warburton, &c.

of the "enfants perdus" partook more of the spirit of the age of chivalry, when every gentleman was required to prove himself worthy of his spurs by individual acts of prowess.

To explain the propriety of here comparing Lear to a "perdu," it may be added, that among other services, that of keeping the night-watches seems to have been a common one. Thus:—

> "—— I have endured
> Another night would trie a 'perdu.'"—*Love and Honour.*

Again:—

> "I am set here like a perdu, to watch a fellow that has wronged my mistress."

ADDENDUM.

> *Fool.* "For you trow, nuncle,
> The hedge-sparrow fed the cuckoo so long,
> That it had its head bit off by its young."
> *Act I. Scene* 4.

This is a remarkable instance of Shakespeare's knowledge of truths of natural history, derived essentially from his own observation; he has exhibited his discrimination between the popular belief and the scientific fact, in this and another notice of the habits of the cuckoo. The fool here expresses the popular belief, which it is natural for a person of his class to participate in, in a proverbial sentence introduced with the usual preface to the introduction of a proverb or trite saying, "for you trow." Worcester, in his address to Henry IV., expresses the scientific fact without falling into the vulgar error—"a fact unnoticed until the time of Dr. Tenner by any writer, except by the naturalist, William Shakespeare."* The passage in Worcester's speech referred to is the following:—

"—— Being fed by us, you us'd us so
As that ungentle gull, the cuckoo's bird,
Useth the sparrow: did oppress our nest;
Grew by our feeding to so great a bulk,
That even our love durst not come near your sight,
For fear of swallowing; but with nimble wing
We were enforc'd, for safety sake, to fly
Out of your sight." . . . . . .

Henry IV. Part I. Act V. Scene 1.

* "Shakespeare; a Biography:" by Charles Knight; where I first found this curious and interesting fact noticed.

Strictly speaking, my task is now concluded. I have carefully selected and illustrated all passages in the play of King Lear which seem to allude to, and throw light upon, the habits, manners, feelings, and superstitions of the times in which Shakespeare lived, confining myself to the antiquarian method of illustration, which the nature of the subject seemed to demand, and carefully avoiding the introduction of any remarks which might be considered irrelevant; but the tendency of these passages has been to give so very unfavourable an idea of the general intellectual condition of this age, that I cannot but think it incumbent on me to endeavour to correct this false impression, by giving a slight sketch which may enable the reader to form a more correct estimate of the real state of society at this period in a moral and intellectual point of view. I have only to add, that should it be considered superfluous (which I would fain hope it will not), the essay may be regarded as complete without it, that which was literally demanded having in fact been already fulfilled.

In the first place, it is to be observed, that the mere circumstance of this age having produced a genius such as Shakespeare, will itself go very far to prove that it must have possessed rare virtues and powers. For it is now a generally acknowledged truth, that when great geniuses appear in this world, as when great inventions are made, it is not merely accidental, but it is to supply some want—to make use of some peculiar capability of their age. This remark may be universally applied, and its truth will at once be evident when we examine it in connexion with any of the great discoveries and inventions which signally benefited mankind—the art of printing, the telescope, the steam engine, the telegraph; and it will be found to hold equally well in this instance. The age had unquestionably a great need of a poet, who might serve as an exponent of the new state of affairs, who might at the same time establish a new school of dramatic poetry in unison with the altered condition of matters, temporal and spiritual, and ennoble and render it permanent by his genius; and who might also prevent the too servile imitation of the literary productions, noble as they were, of an age in which the moral and religious belief fell far below that of his own age, and which productions were therefore in this respect of an inferior level, and so much the more likely to be injurious, if too closely copied, that they were in all other respects of superlative merit. To supply this want Shakespeare arose. The capability of fostering such a genius is as little to be questioned as the need for him. This point will, however, require to be discussed at greater length.

In the sixteenth century England occupied the foremost place among the states of Europe for greatness and importance. The wise administration of Burleigh and Elizabeth enabled the English to prosecute successfully wars in various parts of the globe, chiefly in aid of the reformed religion, while matters at home were but little disturbed. This success, together with the triumphant appeal to the bravery and patriotism of the nation, on the invasion of England by Philip's invincible Armada, had excited a strong feeling of "*amor patriæ*" and of national self-respect. This laudable feeling is manifested in a high degree throughout all the plays of Shakespeare; in fact it pervades the whole of the literature of the age, and gives it not unfrequently a lofty and high-spirited tone, which is very favourable to the spirit of poetry, more especially of that description of poetry which unites a semi-epic character with the dramatic form.

The new discoveries also in remote quarters of the globe, of which the most extravagant and exaggerated accounts were published, afforded a fine field for the play of a poetical imagination. In addition to these accounts of newly-discovered places, the era of which we are treating afforded an abundant crop of voyages and travels; witness the bulky compilations of Hakluyt and Pinchas, in the former of which we have an account of upwards of two hundred voyages, and in the latter the substance of above twelve hundred writers on this subject. But although these must have been of great utility to Shakespeare, and although we find particular and continual traces of them in his works, and more especially of Hakluyt, it nevertheless seems probable that these had by no means so marked an effect as the additions which were now made to the literature of the age in the shape of translations from the Greek and Roman classics. Every classical author of any celebrity was translated into English, with more or less fidelity; the Greek authors, in many instances, from Latin or French versions, but the Roman more generally from the original tongue. Classical literature was much cultivated in this age; Elizabeth was herself a good linguist, better, probably, than any English queen who has succeeded her, and certainly far superior to any who preceded her; her successor, James I., was also a good classical scholar; and people generally, as might be expected under these circumstances, had an excellent knowledge of the classical languages. Nor was fashion the only reason for encouraging the study of these languages, as the following extract from a letter written by Petruccio Ubaldini, in the year 1551, will testify:—"Whoever has the means, has his sons and daughters taught Latin, Greek, and Hebrew; for since the first storm of heresy burst over this land, it has been held necessary for every one to read the scriptures in their original languages."* Thus the general acquaintance with the dead languages was turned to an excellent purpose, and tended to foster and

* Ulrici's "Dramatic Art of Shakespeare," p. 61

encourage that praiseworthy feeling which was one great characteristic of the age—the earnest desire to understand and appreciate the Bible.

This feeling and its results were among the most prominent and the best features of the age; its immediate effects were to induce an earnestness of purpose which distinguishes the serious writers of these times, and is always felt in a greater or less degree by the attentive reader. It impressed the literature of the period with a character of thoughtfulness, and deep, solemn reflection, which is nowhere more apparent than in the works of Shakespeare. But it did more than even this; it promoted and led to a course of free scientific inquiry, founded on the only true basis, which has since occupied the attention of the most intellectual men of all succeeding ages, none of which can, however, boast of a name that stands higher in this branch of literature than does that of Bacon, who though emulated, in his own age, but by few, was nevertheless followed at a distance by Lord Edward of Cherbury, John Barclay, William Gilbert, John Napier, Thomas Harriot, and some others of the same school. With all the refining influences at work which I have indicated, it would be matter for great surprise if we did not find a certain polish and refinement diffused over all classes of society, which rendered them far above the standard of the preceding ages. This was eminently the case both in mind and body. In the latter, it was carried to so great an excess as to become in some persons a considerable abuse, but one which found severe castigators in Prynne, Stubbe, and many other writers of the Puritanical sect, who attacked the inordinate love of dress, and the excessive refinement, degenerating very frequently into effeminacy, with the greatest bitterness. And here again, it may be observed, we have a fine poetical contrast; on the one hand, the stern, gloomy Puritans, standing aloof from every pleasure, every light amusement, and denouncing, in the strongest terms, all who took part in them; and on the other, the light, gay Cavaliers of the court, thinking only of gratifying their appetite for pleasure, and their desire for the continued excitement, by long habit become necessary to them.

Another very remarkable feature in the intellectual history of this period (the last, I believe, on which I shall find it necessary to remark) was the mingling of the spirit and the forms of the middle ages—of the period which had passed—with that of the new era—the age which had just commenced. It is this which gives peculiar propriety to the epithet "picturesque," which has been very judiciously employed to express the effect of this intermingling of the peculiarities of two eras widely dissimilar in character. It was indeed a picturesque age. The stately grandeur, the haughty spirit of exclusiveness, the wild, yet frequently deeply significant superstitions of the middle ages, were slowly melting away before the intellectual vigour and philosophical depth of the new era, which was daily and hourly gaining the ascendency over the minds of men. But while this process was going on, the aspect of the times was a very remarkable one. Chivalry itself, as an institution, was gone; nevertheless, many of its forms still remained, and its influence continued to be felt, in the spirit of gallantry, and of devotion and respect to females, which its laws rigidly and carefully inculcated; albeit, it also left a legacy of covert immorality and profligacy which was a foul stain upon the character of the age. The ancient legends and superstitions, also, were far from being discredited. "The world of spirits, elves, and fairies, magic and witchcraft, astrology and alchemy, and all the secret arts and sciences of the middle ages, still lived in the popular belief, feeding and filling the fancy with their wonderful and poetical imagery."* The old customs, the old festivals, the old games and holidays, were still retained. In short, the fantastic and poetic spirit of the middle ages yet survived in a time which was nevertheless the dawn of a mental tendency directly opposed to it. Thus there was a strong and poetical contrast furnished. All this tended to nourish and foster the spirit of poetry in a high degree; and accordingly this age is marked by a burst of poetic talent, which has rarely, if ever, been equalled.

* "Dramatic Art of Shakespeare," p. 165.

In the history of this country it is certainly unparalleled, and it has but one rival in that of the universe; of this I have already spoken in the introductory remarks which I have prefixed.

I have now, I trust, succeeded in showing that the intellectual merits of this period were many and rare, notwithstanding that the obvious necessity for brevity has prevented me from entering into many particulars, by which the list might have been considerably swelled. Of its defects, I have already had occasion to speak, and need therefore here only remark, that they consisted principally of a certain looseness of morals, profligacy, gaming, and an inordinate love of dress and ostentatious finery generally; the prevalence of swearing, even among women, in whose mouths an oath is both unnatural and discreditable; a lingering belief in the superstitions and impieties of that most superstitious of all periods, the middle ages; and many other vices and follies of greater or less enormity. These are, undoubtedly, considerable defects, but they are, many of them, the faults of a great age; some of them, indeed, were merely the degrading legacy of the preceding ages of comparative intellectual darkness, but others were the result of that exuberant vigour and energy which was so eminently the characteristic of the times. I think that, on the whole, weighing the merits of the age against its demerits, it will be confessed by all that the balance is *very greatly* in favour of the former. At the least, no one can refuse to look upon that age as an eminently glorious one, which has contributed to the list of the literary and scientific benefactors of our country and of the whole world, names such as those of Bacon, Raleigh, Napier, Harriot, Donne, Hales, Pyne, Sidney, Spenser, Abraham Cowley, Green, Peele, Marlowe, Jonson, Beaumont and Fletcher, Massinger, Chapman, Decker, and—greatest of all—Shakespeare!

FINIS.

List of Works used or referred to in the course of this Essay, and containing useful information on its subject.

1. Dr. Drake's Shakespeare and his Times.

2. Douce's Illustrations of Shakespeare.

3. Knight's Edition (Pictorial) of Shakespeare.

4. Notes to the Variorum Edition of Shakespeare; including Notes by Johnson, Steevens, Malone, Capell, Warburton, Theobald, Hanmer, Jennens, Ritson, *et alii multi.*

5. Knight's Shakespeare; a Biography.

6. Romantic Biography of the Age of Elizabeth, by Dr. Cooke Taylor. Article, Life of Dr. Dee.

7. Nare's Glossary of Obsolete Words.

8. Pye's Commentary on Shakespeare.

9. Strutt's Sports and Pastimes of the People of England.

10. Armin's Nest of Ninnies (Shakespeare Society); with Introduction and Notes, by Mr. P. Collier and Mr. Thoms.

11. London Magazine, Vols. II., III., IV., &c. (Taylor and Hessey.)

12. Ulrici's Dramatic Art of Shakespeare. Part II., Shakespeare and his Times.

13. Stubbe's Anatomie of Abuses, and View of Vanitie.

14. Eccles's Edition of the Plays of King Lear and Cymbeline (1801).

15. Harrison's Description of England; published with Hollinshed's Chronicle.

16. New Illustrations of the Life and Studies of Shakespeare, by the Rev. T. Hunter, F.S.A., &c.

17. Aubrey's Manuscript History of Wiltshire.

18. Dr. Harsnet's Declaration of Egregious Popish Impostures, published in 1603; &c., &c.

Breinigsville, PA USA
04 March 2011
257012BV00003B/72/A